3/96

IMAGES ACROSS THE AGES

JAPANESE PORTRAITS

Dorothy
and
Thomas Hoobler

Illustrations by
Victoria Bruck

RSVP

RAINTREE
STECK-VAUGHN
PUBLISHERS
The Steck-Vaughn Company

Austin, Texas

Cover and interior design: Suzanne Beck
Electronic Production: Scott Melcer
Project Manager: Joyce Spicer

Library of Congress Cataloging-in-Publication Data
Hoobler, Dorothy.
    Japanese portraits / by Dorothy and Thomas Hoobler : illustrated by Victoria Bruck.
       p.   cm. — (Images across the ages)
    Includes bibliographical references and index.
    ISBN 0-8114-6381-8
    1. Japan — Biography.   I. Hoobler, Thomas.   II. Bruck,Victoria, ill.
III. Title.   IV. Series: Hoobler, Dorothy. Images across the ages
DS834.H66   1994
920.052—dc20   93-39627
[B]   CIP AC

Printed and bound in the United States by Lake Book, Melrose Park, IL
1 2 3 4 5 6 7 8 9 0 LB 98 97 96 95 94 93

CONTENTS

INTRODUCTION

A DIVINE LAND

The Japanese people have a legend about the divine creation of the islands of their homeland. Long ago two *kami*, or gods, Izanami and her brother Izanagi, stood looking over the rainbow bridge that separated the heavens from earth. Reaching down, Izanagi dipped a long spear into the churning waters below. When he removed the spear, drops of salty water fell from the spear's tip and formed land. The divine brother and sister then descended and created other kami.

In giving birth to fire, Izanami was so badly burned that she went to the underworld or the Land of Death. Grief-stricken, Izanagi later searched for her there. But when he found his sister's rotting corpse, he fled in horror. To wash away the uncleanliness of death, Izanagi purified himself in a river. While bathing, he gave birth to the two most powerful kami—Amaterasu the Sun Goddess and Susanoo the god of the oceans.

Trouble soon brewed in paradise. Amaterasu shone her light and warmth across the high plain of heaven. Her brother Susanoo, however, turned out to be boisterous and wild. "This god had a fierce temper," according to an early Japanese story, "and was given to cruel acts. Moreover, he made a practice of continually weeping and wailing." In heaven, Susanoo rampaged through Amaterasu's rice fields, trampling the dikes and washing away the seedlings. He tracked dirt through her palace and ruined her weaving room by throwing a horse through the roof. This was too much for Amaterasu. She hid in a cave and refused to come out.

Now there was no sunlight; heaven and earth were plunged into darkness. The other kami pleaded with Amaterasu, but in vain. To lure her out, the kami placed a mirror in front of the cave and began a riotous party. But Amaterasu ignored their singing and dancing until one kami performed a funny and sexy dance. Amaterasu's curiosity was aroused by the uproarious laughter. She peeked out and saw her own reflection in the mirror. When she edged forward to take a closer look, the kami dragged her out. Light was restored to the world.

The Sun Goddess looked down on the "land of luxuriant rice fields," and sent her grandson, Ninigi, to govern Japan. She commanded him: "Do thou, my August Grandchild, proceed thither and govern it. Go! and may prosperity attend thy dynasty, and may it, like Heaven and Earth, endure forever." Amaterasu gave Ninigi three gifts—a sword, the mirror that had drawn her from the cave, and a curved jewel.

Ninigi landed at Kyushu, the southernmost of Japan's four large islands, and ruled it well. His grandson, Jimmu, moved onto the largest island, Honshu, using the sword to conquer the inhabitants who refused to accept his rule. Jimmu set up his kingdom on the Yamato Plain south of today's city of Nara.

Here Jimmu offered sacrifices to the Sun Goddess and declared himself the emperor of Japan. According to tradition, this happened in the year 660 B.C. Jimmu was the first of a long line of emperors that continues to this day. Each new emperor receives the sword, jewel, and mirror —called the imperial regalia. They are the symbols of his right to rule.

These and other legends formed an important part of the ancient Japanese religion called Shinto. Shinto is a simple belief in nature worship. Spirits or gods, the kami, live everywhere—in rivers, caves, mountains, and rocks. The Sun Goddess is only the most powerful example.

Shinto has no sacred books and few commandments. Cleanliness and sincerity are its most important values. Worship takes place in simple shrines that dot the countryside and are even found in modern office buildings. Devotees purify themselves by washing before they approach a shrine. Then they clap hands twice to get the attention of the kami. The holiest spot in Japan is the Shrine of Amaterasu, at Ise, where her sacred mirror is kept. Amaterasu's spirit is believed to reside within it.

Over the centuries, the Japanese have welcomed religious ideas from elsewhere. But the Shinto ideals endured. A deep sense of awe for nature fostered a keen appreciation of beauty. This love of natural beauty has found expression in Japanese art and everyday life throughout the country's history.

THE PRINCE OF SACRED VIRTUE—
SHOTOKU TAICHI

In A.D. 574, the empress of Japan had a vision. Because it was the first day of the new year, it was a lucky day for her country. A priest, surrounded by golden light, appeared to the empress. He asked that she allow a god to live in her womb so that he could be born as a human being. The empress agreed.

As the year progressed, she prepared to give birth. On the day of her delivery, she left the living quarters of the palace. Japanese believed that giving birth made a home impure. As she was passing the palace stables, she gave birth to a boy without any effort at all.

From the very beginning, this prince was special. According to an ancient chronicle of Japan, "He was able to speak as soon as he was born, and so wise when he grew up that he could attend to the suits [law cases] of ten men at once and decide them all without error. He knew beforehand what was going to happen."

The names of the prince reflected his birth and amazing feats. In Japan, an individual often had many names over a lifetime, and sometimes received a new one after his death. The newborn prince was called Umayado, which means "Stable Door," from his place of birth. A later name was Toyotomimi or "Abundant Quick Ears," in recognition of his ability to listen to the "ten suits at a time." In history, he is best known as Shotoku Taichi or Prince Shotoku. The name means Sacred Virtue, and was bestowed on him after his death. It was appropriate. For Prince Shotoku was destined to become one of the most important figures in Japanese history.

When Prince Shotoku was born, Japan was on the brink of great changes. At the time, Japan was backward in comparison with its neighbors China and Korea. Both of these countries had a written language, high art, and strong governments. Japan did not.

Over the centuries, wars on the mainland of Asia brought some Korean and Chinese refugees to Japan. From them, the Japanese learned of their neighbors' accomplishments.

Japan was ruled by many powerful clans who held sway over different parts of the country. The emperor was only the most respected of the clan leaders. His claim to descent from Amaterasu enabled him to perform certain religious duties on behalf of the whole country.

In 552, during the reign of Shotoku's grandfather, ambassadors from a Korean kingdom visited Japan. The Koreans brought a golden image of the Buddha with a letter from their king recommending the Buddhist religion. "This religion is the most excellent of all teachings," the letter read. "Though difficult to master and hard to comprehend....It brings endless and immeasurable blessings and fruits....the Treasures of the glorious religion will never cease to give full response to those who seek for it."

Buddhism was already 1,000 years old when it reached Japan. The religion was based on the teachings of Siddhartha Gautama of India (known as the Buddha, or "Enlightened One.") The Buddha preached that people could end human suffering by following an "eightfold path" of ethical conduct and meditation. The goal of the "eightfold path" was enlightenment—that sudden insight into truth that first came to the Buddha himself. Over the centuries, Buddhist followers had developed a rich art, profound literature, and spiritual practices to help believers toward their goal.

The Korean king's gift provoked a debate within Japan. Should the country adopt the new foreign religion? Some leaders said yes; others no. "Why should we revere strange deities, and turn our backs upon the gods of our country?" said one opponent.

The Soga clan became the leaders of the pro-Buddhist faction. They built a Buddhist shrine on their family estate, but then a plague broke out in Japan, and the new religion was blamed. The Sogas' shrine was destroyed. But when the disease continued to spread, the Sogas asked to restore the shrine. They argued that the Buddha was angry because the religion had not been accepted.

The dispute continued throughout Shotoku's childhood, coming to a head when he was about 13. In 587, the Sogas made war on the anti-Buddhist clans. Young Prince Shotoku joined the Soga forces and played a key role in the battle. When the other side

8

seemed about to win, Shotoku quickly cut down a tree. From the wood, he formed four Buddhist images that he placed in his top-knot of hair. He vowed that if the Soga forces were triumphant, he would build a temple to the Buddha. This seems to have gained the Buddha's favor, for the tide of battle turned and the Soga forces won.

In 592, the emperor died and Shotoku's aunt, known as Suiko, took the throne. In those times, women could become *tenno*, or emperor. Suiko was known for her beauty and skills in cooking. She was a devout Buddhist and the following year, she decided to become a nun. Shotoku was named imperial prince. Though he never held the title of tenno, he controlled the government and acted in his aunt's name.

The prince began to study Buddhism more deeply with a Korean priest. He also studied the Confucian classics. These books contained the ideas of Confucius, a Chinese philosopher who had lived about the same time as the Buddha. Confucius stressed the importance of obedience to superiors. Sons should revere and obey their fathers. Wives must obey their husbands. In the same way, the people should treat the emperor as the father of the nation.

Confucius' thoughts on government and ethics had a great influence within China. The Chinese emperors adopted Confucianism as the state philosophy. For centuries, China's strong central government had helped to create a great civilization.

Shotoku was amazed by the many accomplishments of the Chinese. He learned to read and write the Chinese language. He learned about Chinese astronomy, geography, mathematics, and poetry. He was excited by these wondrous discoveries. Here was the knowledge that would modernize Japan. His fondest wish was to bring the greatness of Chinese culture to Japan.

Shotoku set to work. In 604, he took a step toward building a powerful central government. He prepared the Seventeen Article Constitution, Japan's first code of laws.

This "constitution" was different from what we today would think of as a legal code. Instead of naming specific rules, it set forth general moral and ethical principles. For example, it began with the statement, "Harmony is to be valued." The prince's idealism shone forth in Article 10:

Let us cease from wrath and refrain from angry looks. Nor let us be resentful when others differ from us. For all men have hearts and each heart has its own leanings. Their right is our wrong and our right is their wrong. We are not unquestionably sages, nor are they unquestionably fools. Both of us are simply ordinary men. How can any man lay down a rule by which to distinguish right from wrong? For we are all, one with another, wise and foolish, like a ring which has no end....

The constitution called for ministers to obey the lead of the emperor. It set forth proper behavior, such as avoiding gluttony or overeating. It advised attending court early in the morning, and avoiding pettiness and envy.

Shotoku clearly took his inspiration from Confucian ideas. But the document also stated that "reverence should be accorded to Buddhism." Aristocrats seeking to gain favor with Shotoku built temples, pagodas, and shrines throughout the land. Still, the Japanese continued to follow Shinto as well. Over the years, the two religions would become closely entwined.

Prince Shotoku realized that Japan had even more to learn. He started sending Japanese educational missions to China to study the source of its civilization. Shotoku's missions to China began an era of cultural borrowing by the Japanese. For the next two centuries, students and priests made the difficult and often dangerous journey.

The Japanese proved adept learners. Many of the Chinese cultural customs became part of the Japanese heritage. Japan adopted Chinese writing, court ritual, and calendar. Devotion to Buddhism created a flowering of religious art modeled on Chinese styles. Not until the arrival of ships from the United States (more than 1,300 years later), would Japan be so open to outside influences.

From this time, the Japanese adopted a new name for their nation. Formerly, they had called their land Yamato, but now they used Nihon or Nippon, a word that combines the Chinese characters for "sun" and "source." Centuries later, when the Italian Marco Polo visited China, he heard the Chinese pronunciation of this name: "Jihpen." Polo's book about his travels brought the name Japan to the West.

Prince Shotoku himself worked and studied at his home at the Palace of Ikaruga on the Yamato River. He kept the vow he had made while fighting with the Soga clan. Next to his home, he constructed the Horyuji, the oldest Buddhist temple complex in Japan. Although it burned down after his death, a replica soon replaced it. Still standing today, the Horyuji contains the oldest wooden buildings in the world. In his last years, the prince was working on a national history of Japan. Unfortunately it has not survived the ravages of time.

He died at Ikaruga in the middle of the night around the year 623. He was less than 50 years old. A great sadness descended over the land. A chronicler wrote:

> At this time all the Princes and Imperial Chieftains, as well as the people of the empire, the old, as if they had lost a dear child, had no taste for salt or vinegar in their mouths; the young, as if they had lost a beloved parent, filled the ways with the sound of their lamenting. The farmer ceased from his plow, and the pounding woman laid down her pestle. They all said: "The sun and moon have lost their brightness; heaven and earth have crumbled to ruin: henceforward, in whom shall we put our trust?"

Prince Shotoku is one of the most beloved figures in Japanese history. He is admired for sponsoring the adoption of the high culture of China, which is so important a part of the Japanese heritage. For his devotion to Buddhism, many revere him as a saint. His face today is perhaps the best known of Japan's historical figures. Until recently, it appeared on the 10,000-yen note, guaranteeing its value. With Shotoku, Japanese culture begins.

DWELLERS AMONG THE CLOUDS—
MURASAKI SHIKIBU AND
SEI SHONAGON

A very proud person. She values herself highly, and scatters her Chinese writings all about. Yet should we study her closely, we should find that she is still imperfect. She tries to be exceptional, but naturally persons of that sort give offense. She is piling up trouble for her future. One who is too richly gifted, who indulges too much in emotion...in spite of herself will lose self-control. How can such a vain and reckless person end her days happily?

This perceptive criticism was written in the diary of Lady Murasaki Shikibu in the first years of the 11th century. She was writing about Sei Shonagon, a woman who, like herself, was a member of the Japanese court society. From the outside, life at court looked lavish and pleasurable. To those within, it was often filled with backbiting, gossip, and envy.

The two women were a study in contrasts. Sei Shonagon was vivacious and bold. In her writings, she often skewered rivals savagely. Lady Murasaki, on the other hand, was shy and self-conscious. Murasaki criticized herself in her diary with the same unblinking honesty:

Having no excellence within myself, I have passed my days without making any special impression on anyone. Especially the fact that I have no man who will look out for my future makes me comfortless. I do not wish to bury myself in dreariness. Is it because of my worldly mind that I feel lonely? On moonlight nights in autumn, when I am hopelessly sad, I often go out on the balcony and gaze dreamily at the moon. It makes me think of days gone by. People say that it is dangerous to look at the moon in solitude, but something impels me, and sit-

ting a little withdrawn I muse there. In the wind-cooled evening I play on the koto [a stringed instrument], though others may not care to hear it. I fear that my playing betrays the sorrow which becomes more intense, and I become disgusted with myself—so foolish and miserable am I.

Lady Murasaki's critical self-appraisal gives no hint of her gifts. She is the author of Japan's greatest novel, *The Tale of Genji*, one of the world's literary masterpieces. Sei Shonagon's own writing, in *The Pillow Book*, sparkles and brings her times to life. The two women were the greatest writers of a remarkable era.

The two court ladies, Murasaki and Shonagon, lived in Heian-kyo—"the Capital of Peace and Tranquility." Heian-kyo, today's Kyoto, became Japan's capital in 794. Here the Japanese gained cultural assurance. The study missions to China stopped. Though the Japanese retained a high respect for Chinese culture, over time they began to develop one that was uniquely their own.

An example was the creation of the *kana* in the ninth century. Kana is a simplified version of the Chinese written characters. It is used like an alphabet, but instead of letters, there are 50 syllables corresponding to Japanese sounds. The kana became popular among women. But court officials and most males preferred Chinese. They called kana "women's writing." Yet Sei Shonagon and Lady Murasaki, writing in kana, created works that are among the glories of Japanese literature.

The small number of people who lived within the Heian court called themselves "dwellers among the clouds." Perhaps never before or since have people taken such delight in the pursuit of beauty. People were judged by their ability to write poetry and by the quality of their handwriting, or calligraphy. It was not unusual for someone to fall in love just from seeing another person's work with the brush used for writing. Letter writing was a passion. Even the quality of the paper was regarded as an indication of taste.

These "dwellers" took a very competitive approach to beauty. Among their favorite amusements were contests in mixing perfume scents. Teams would cooperate in painting beautiful scrolls, asking a judge to decide which was best. Members of the court sometimes gathered on the bank of a river. One would write the first line of a poem and send it floating downstream. The person who picked it from the water had to write the next line of the poem, and so on.

Standards of personal beauty were just as high, though they were quite different from today's ideals. Both sexes wore white facial powder. They blackened their teeth—white teeth were considered vulgar. Women shaved their eyebrows and painted false ones high on their foreheads. A fashionable woman's crowning glory was her long lustrous black hair which often fell to below her feet.

People of the court loved gorgeous clothing. Sei Shonagon describes the outfit of one courtier:

> His resplendent, cherry-colored Court cloak was lined with material of the most delightful hue and lustre; he wore dark, grape-colored trousers, boldly splashed with designs of wisteria branches; his crimson under-robe was so glossy that it seemed to sparkle, while underneath one could make out layer upon layer of white and light violet robes.

Women wore as many as 12 layers of robes in different colors. Different lengths at the neck and cuffs showed each fabric. Woe to the person who mixed and matched her clothing badly. Lady Murasaki remarks in her diary:

> On that day all the ladies in attendance on His Majesty had taken particular care with their dress. One of them, however, had made a small error in matching the colors at the openings of the sleeves. When she approached His Majesty to put something in order, the High Court Nobles and Senior Courtiers who were standing nearby noticed the mistake and stared at her....It was not really such a serious lapse of taste; only the color of one of her robes was a shade too pale at the opening.

The emperor presided over this splendid court, but real power was held by the Fujiwara family. By providing their daughters as wives for the emperors, the Fujiwara aristocrats linked their family to the throne. Through their daughters and grandchildren, the Fujiwaras came to rule in the emperor's name. The emperor Ichijo, who reigned from 986 to 1011, was an example. He had two major wives—both members of the Fujiwara clan. Sei Shonagon served at the court of the first and Lady Murasaki at the court of the second.

Sei Shonagon was born sometime in the 960s to a family that traced its ancestry back to an early emperor. Her father was one of the "five poets of the Pear Court" and had edited an important collection of poetry for the emperor. As a girl, Shonagon showed a talent for writing and scholarship. She learned the Chinese classics and wrote poetry. When she was about 30, in the year 992, she became the lady-in-waiting to the young empress Sadako.

Sei Shonagon's learning enabled her to hold her own with the male courtiers. The empress, then only about 14, was proud of Shonagon's achievements, and the two became close friends. Indeed, it was the empress who provided Shonagon with the paper she used to begin her famous *Pillow Book*.

"I now had a vast quantity of paper at my disposal," Sei Shonagon wrote,

> and I set about filling the notebooks with odd facts, stories from the past, and all sorts of other things, often including the most trivial material. On the whole I concentrated on things and people that I found charming and splendid.

The Pillow Book got its name from the fact that Shonagon kept her jottings near at hand, sometimes under her wooden pillow. This collection of observations is a popular kind of writing in Japan where it is called "following the brush." Shonagon's book is the finest example. It opens with what she liked best about the seasons:

> In spring it is the dawn that is most beautiful. As the light creeps over the hills, their outlines are dyed a faint red and wisps of purplish cloud trail over them.
>
> In summer the nights. Not only when the moon shines, but on dark nights too, as the fireflies flit to and fro, and even when it rains, how beautiful it is!
>
> In autumn the evenings, when the glittering sun sinks close to the edge of the hills and the crows fly back to their nests in threes and fours and twos; more charming still is a file of wild geese, like specks in the distant sky. When the sun has set, one's heart is moved by the sound of the wind and the hum of the insects.
>
> In winter the early mornings. It is beautiful indeed when snow has fallen during the night, but splendid too when the ground is white with frost; or even when there is no snow or frost, but it is simply very cold and the attendants hurry from room to room stirring up the fires and bringing charcoal, how well this fits the season's mood! But as noon approaches and the cold wears off, no one bothers to keep the braziers alight, and soon nothing remains but piles of white ashes.

Sometimes she recounted amusing incidents, like the following, in which she poked fun at a courtier:

> One day when he thought he was alone in the Table Room, neither of the First Secretaries having reported for duty, Masahiro took a dish of beans that was lying there and went behind the Little Screen. Suddenly someone pulled aside the screen—and there was Masahiro, stealthily munching away at the beans. Everyone who saw him was convulsed with laughter.

At other times, Shonagon gives random personal opinions, such as her list of "hateful things":

> One has gone to bed and is about to doze off when a mosquito appears, announcing himself in a reedy voice. One can actually feel the wind made by his wings and, slight though it is, one finds it hateful in the extreme.
> A carriage passes with a nasty, creaking noise. Annoying to think that the passengers may not even be aware of this! If I am travelling in someone's carriage and I hear it creaking, I dislike not only the noise but also the owner of the carriage.

Shonagon could be quite mean when she wrote of others, and the common people were no exception. She viewed them almost as a different species. Visiting a temple, she wrote:

> I hurried into my enclosure, longing to gaze upon the sacred countenance of Buddha. To my dismay I found that a throng of commoners had settled themselves directly in front of me, where they were incessantly standing up, prostrating themselves, and squatting down again. They looked like so many basket-worms as they crowded together in their hideous clothes, leaving hardly an inch of space between themselves and me. I really felt like pushing them all over sideways.

Sei Shonagon's sharp tongue earned her enemies at court. She was once reproached for being the only member of the court not to compose a poem for a contest, though she was the daughter of a master. She may have been boastful, as Lady Murasaki claims in her diary. Others at court criticized her as arrogant and she was accused of drinking more than was proper for a lady.

After the death of the empress in the year 1001, Shonagon retired to a modest house. Those who had been stung by her remarks had not forgotten her. Sometimes young courtiers came to heckle her, calling out, "Shonagon has fallen that low." Years later an attendant of the succeeding court wrote, "In the neighborhood of her father's home lives Sei Shonagon. The snow fell heavily upon the wall surrounding her home and under the burden of the snow, it crumbled until nothing of it remains." After the attendant's visit, Sei Shonagon made this note: "After aging and during a life of seclusion meeting no one, someone came to call upon me."

To the court of Ichijo's second empress, Lady Akiko, came Murasaki Shikabu. About 10 years younger than Sei Shonagon, Lady Murasaki was born in the 970s. She too came from a distinguished background; both her parents were Fujiwaras. As a girl, she showed signs of great talent. She recalled:

> When my elder brother was a boy he was taught to read the Chinese classics. I listened, sitting beside him, and learned wonderfully fast, though he was sometimes slow and forgot. Father, who was devoted to study, regretted that I had not been a son, but I heard people saying that it is not beautiful even for a man to be proud of his learning, and after that I did not write so much as the figure one in Chinese. I grew clumsy with my writing brush. For a long time I did not care for the books I had already read.

When Murasaki was 18 she accompanied her father to his new post as governor of Echizen province. To Heian aristocrats, leaving the capital was regarded almost like going into exile. Murasaki returned to get married before her father's term was finished.

Already in her mid-20s, Murasaki was old for a first marriage. Her husband, 25 years her senior, was a distant relative. After giving birth to a daughter, Murasaki's joy was crushed when her husband died shortly after. Murasaki considered becoming a nun, but realized that her duty to her child prevented that. At this low point in her life, she started writing her masterpiece, *The Tale of Genji*.

Then she entered the court of Lady Akiko. The bookish Murasaki sometimes felt out of place with the younger women at the court. In her diary, she wrote, "Do they really look on me as such a dull thing, I wonder? But I am what I am and so act accordingly. Her Majesty too has often remarked that she had thought I was not the kind of person with whom one could ever relax."

In a short time, however, the empress discovered Murasaki's good qualities, and "I became closer to her than any of the others." Lady Akiko was impressed by Murasaki's knowledge of the Confucian classics, and persuaded Murasaki to give her private lessons. This was done in secret because Chinese learning was usually regarded as a male pursuit.

Often Murasaki found the frivolous activities of the court not to her liking. Her diary shows a strong religious bent:

> I wish I could be more adaptable and live more gaily in the present world—had I not an extraordinary sorrow—but whenever I hear delightful or interesting things my yearning for a religious life grows stronger. I become melancholy and lament. I try to forget, for sorrow is vain. Am I too sinful?

To escape her cares, she threw herself into working on her novel. Someone found the manuscript and passed it around the court. To Murasaki's surprise, the courtiers became interested in the ongoing story. When the emperor heard some of it read aloud, he praised it highly, saying, "She is gifted, she must have read the Chronicle of Japan." This aroused the jealousy of another court lady who accused Murasaki of being too proud, sarcastically calling her "The Japanese Chronicle Lady." Murasaki noted in her diary that this was "laughable, indeed! I am reserved even before the maids of my house; how then should I show my learning in court?"

The Tale of Genji tells of the adventures and spiritual growth of

Genji, "the Shining Prince." Genji represents all the ideals of Heian society. Physically beautiful, he is a fine poet, accomplished musician, and a gallant lover. He pursues beauty in all its forms. Most of all, Genji is touched by the most important Heian sentiment — *aware* (ah-wah-ray).

Aware is the pathos or sorrow that one feels on beholding beautiful things—for one comes to realize that beauty cannot last. Indeed, it is precisely this short-lived character that makes things most beautiful. For example, the Japanese—even today—love to view the blooming of the cherry trees in spring. Though the blossoms cover the trees, they last for only a few days. The same is true of the autumn leaves and the harvest moon that shines on a single night each year. *Aware* combines a love of beauty with the strong Buddhist belief that all things are fleeting.

A passage from the novel describes the effect of its hero practicing a dance before the court:

> As Genji danced, the rays of the setting sun fell on his body, and at that moment the music swelled up in a crescendo. It was a brilliant climax....Moved beyond words by the beauty of the performance, the Emperor burst into tears, and the High Court Nobles and princes in his suite also wept. When the song was finished, Genji adjusted the sleeves of his robe and waited for the music to start again. Then he resumed his dance to the lively strains of the next movement. Excited by the rhythm of the steps, he glowed with a warm color, and the name "Genji the shining One" seemed even more fitting than usual.

Lady Murasaki uses a character in the novel to explain why she created her great work:

> ...it happens because the storyteller's own experience of men and things, whether for good or ill...has moved him to an emotion so passionate that he can no longer keep it shut up in his heart. Again and again something in his own life or that around him will seem to the writer so important that he cannot bear to let it pass into oblivion.

Murasaki's story did not pass into oblivion. Her novel is read and enjoyed throughout the world 900 years after her death. So is *The Pillow Book* of Sei Shonagon. Through their words, the glittering world of the Heian-kyo court lives on.

CHAPTER 3

A TALE OF TWO BROTHERS— YORITOMO AND YOSHITSUNE

Flames swept through the splendid Sanjo Palace in the heart of Kyoto. In the midst of the blazing inferno, swords flashed as warriors of Japan's two strongest clans, the Minamoto and the Taira, fought each other. The year was 1159. Yoshitomo, head of the fierce Minamoto clan, was trying to take control of the capital city from his rival, Kiyomori, leader of the Taira. The fight seesawed back and forth with Japan's fate in the balance.

While the elegant courtiers had been sniffing perfume, they left the governing of the provinces to the warrior clans. Over time, the Minamoto emerged as the strongest clan in the eastern part of the country. The Taira were supreme in the west and around the Inland Sea.

A dispute over the succession to the imperial throne brought the warriors, called *samurai*, into the capital city. Court supporters of each would-be emperor sought help from one of the competing clans. In the fighting that followed, the cultured and gentle courtiers saw their power swept away. Aristocrats desperately tried to flee in their ox-drawn carriages. Many of Kyoto's beautiful homes and buildings were destroyed.

When the Taira proved too strong, the Minamoto forces retreated from the city in the winter of 1160. Yoshitomo's oldest son was wounded and floundered in the snow. Dreading the shame of being captured and not wishing to hold up the others, he begged to be killed. His father did the deed himself. A short time later, Yoshitomo too was slain—in his bathtub by a treacherous retainer. Without him, the rest of the Minamoto forces were soon defeated.

But Kiyomori, in an uncharacteristic act of charity, decided to spare the two younger sons of his enemy. They were Yoritomo, who was about 13 at the time, and Yoshitsune, only an infant. It was a

fateful decision for both the Taira and Japan. Twenty years later, the two young Minamotos would reappear.

Minamoto Yoritomo was born in Kyoto in 1147 and spent his childhood in the city. Fighting on the battlefield beside his great father, he shared in the shame of defeat. To avenge it was his secret dream during his young years. He was sent into exile on the Izu Peninsula in the lands of the Hojo family.

Originally treated as a political prisoner, Yoritomo soon won the regard of the Hojo lord. The daughter of the family, Hojo Masako, took a decided liking to the young man. She was head-strong and bold—a worthy daughter of a warrior. The two ran off and married on the eve of her arranged marriage to another suitor. After his initial anger cooled, Masako's father accepted the situation and became one of his son-in-law's greatest supporters.

During his exile, Yoritomo kept himself informed of events in Kyoto. Taira Kiyomori ruled much as the Fujiwara had before. He married one of his daughters into the imperial family. Her son, Antoku, was named emperor as an infant. But Kiyomori's arrogance made him unpopular, and at the same time the country suffered from famine and floods, further destroying his support.

By the end of 1180, Yoritomo was ready to strike. He raised the flag of revolt against Kiyomori. The Taira leader sent a large army against him, one that vastly outnumbered Yoritomo's own force. The two samurai armies gathered on either side of the Fujikawa River. Mount Fuji, Japan's most famous mountain, overlooked the scene on the plain below.

A stroke of fate brought Yoritomo good luck. One of his scouts, moving through a marsh on the riverbank, disturbed a large flock of geese. Thousands of birds flew into the air all at once. The noise of their wings sounded like hoofbeats to the Taira soldiers. Believing they were about to be attacked by a larger force, the Tairas beat a hasty retreat. Yoritomo was left in control of the plain.

A few months later, Taira Kiyomori died in Kyoto. According to legend, he gathered his sons around him on his deathbed, and made them promise that they would carry on the fight. They pledged to leave Yoritomo's corpse rotting on the ground.

Yoritomo made no immediate effort to follow up his surprising victory because he had not secured his position in the east. He set up his headquarters at Kamakura, south of today's Tokyo. Here he gave thanks at the shrine of Hachiman, the Shinto god of war.

One day, a gallant young man came riding into Yoritomo's camp. It was his brother Yoshitsune; Yoritomo had not seen him in 20 years. As a baby, Yoshitsune had been taken to a monastery, where, on Kiyomori's orders, he was raised to become a monk. But even as a child he was attracted to the sword and the bow. According to legend, he was trained in the arts of war by a *tengu*, a kind of mythical super-warrior. In his teens, Yoshitsune fled the monastery, determined to avenge his father. Hearing of his brother's victory, he went to join him.

Yoritomo at once recognized Yoshitsune's superb skills as a warrior, and put him in charge of a Minamoto army. Yoshitsune marched to the west, eager to defeat the Taira forces. In February 1184, he led his warriors to the first of three famous victories. Before the battle, the Taira held an apparently impregnable position on a narrow strip of land between the mountains and the Inland Sea. If Yoshitsune attacked them head-on, his men would be cut to pieces.

But Yoshitsune acted with boldness and daring. In the middle of the night, he led a small number of his men on horseback to a ridge that overlooked the Taira camp. At daybreak, the rest of Yoshitsune's forces launched a frontal attack; the Taira rushed to meet it. Suddenly, Yoshitsune's horsemen came storming down the ridge in the Taira's rear. So steep was the slope that the attackers closed their eyes as they spurred their horses down the cliffside.

The Tairas were routed. The survivors fled across the Inland Sea to their headquarters at Yashima on the northern shore of Shikoku Island. Along with them the Tairas brought the infant emperor Antoku and the imperial regalia.

Once more, the Taira took up a position that they believed Yoshitsune could not overrun. Indeed, a year passed before the next battle. Yoshitsune's officers advised him against an attack, but he believed surprise and boldness would again carry the day. During a storm, he and his best soldiers crossed the Inland Sea in small boats. Yoshitsune calculated that the wind would increase their speed. In the dead of night he and his soldiers reached the opposite shore and quickly marched to the Taira camp.

Although Yoshitsune's men were greatly outnumbered, they had the advantage of surprise. At dawn, they launched their attack,

setting fire to the houses in the region. With the flames rising
behind them, they rushed into the midst of the Taira forces. Many
surrendered in the panic. Others fled to the sea where their boats
awaited. According to a Japanese chronicle of the war:

> Elated with victory, the [Minamoto] rode into the sea in pursuit
> till they were up to their saddles in water and fought among
> the ships, while the [Taira] with rakes and billhooks tried to
> seize Yoshitsune by the neckpiece of his helmet. Two or three
> times their weapons rattled above his head, but his companions
> with sword and halberd warded off the attacks from their mas-
> ter as they fought. In the course of the fighting [Yoshitsune]
> somehow or other dropped his bow into the sea, and leant out
> of the saddle trying to pick it up again with his whip. His com-
> panions cried out to him to let it go, but he would not, and at
> last managed to recover it, and rode back laughing to the beach.

The surviving Taira made their escape, again taking the child
emperor and his grandmother with them. The final battle was
fought at sea off Dannoura on the western shore of Honshu Island.
According to the chronicle, "Both sides set their faces against each
other and fought grimly without a thought for their lives, neither
giving an inch." Although the Taira had more experience in naval

battles, luck again rode with the Minamoto. At first the Taira ships forced the Minamoto back. But then the tide changed and began to flow toward the land, sweeping the Taira fleet onto the rocky shore.

As the warriors on both sides watched, the ship carrying the emperor began to sink. The chronicle tells what happened:

> The Emperor was seven years old that year....He was so lovely that he seemed to shed a brilliant radiance about him, and his long black hair hung loose far down his back. With a look of surprise and anxiety on his face he asked the Lady Nii [his grandmother], "Where are you going to take me?"
>
> She turned to the youthful sovereign, with tears streaming down her cheeks....She comforted him, and bound up his long hair in his dove-colored robe. Blinded with tears, the child sovereign put his beautiful little hands together. He turned to the east to say farewell to the deity of Ise....The Lady Nii took him tightly in her arms and with the words, "In the depths of the ocean is our capital," sank with him at last beneath the waves.

Antoku and his grandmother drowned, carrying the three sacred regalia with them to the bottom. Later, the mirror and the jewel were recovered, but the ancient sword was never found. The one that is given to today's emperor is a replica.

Yoshitsune's victory message to his brother said it all: "On the twenty-fourth day of the Third Month at the Hour of the Hare at Dannoura in the Province of Nagato...the Taira were annihilated. The Sacred Mirror and the Sacred Jewel are being safely returned to the Capital."

However, Yoritomo did not feel grateful for his brother's victory. The seeds of jealousy had taken root within his heart. When Yoshitsune arrived at Kyoto, he was treated as a hero. The news aroused Yoritomo's suspicions, and he refused to meet his brother when he arrived at Kamakura. Yoshitsune wrote a letter to his brother: "Here am I, weeping crimson tears in vain at thy displeasure....These many days I have lain here and could not gaze upon thy face. The bond of our bloodbrotherhood is sundered...."

In response, Yoritomo stripped his brother of all his titles. Yoshitsune learned that assassins had been sent to kill him. Rather than wage war against his brother, Yoshitsune fled from place to place. Now he needed all his military skills to survive. He was the most wanted man in Japan.

Yoshitsune's pregnant mistress Shizuka could not keep up with him and returned to Kyoto. She was captured and sent to Yoritomo. Known as the most beautiful dancer in Japan, she was forced to dance for Yoritomo outside the shrine of Hachiman. She defied him by dancing and singing in honor of Yoshitsune. Only the pleas of Masako, Yoritomo's wife, saved her life. Later, when Shizuka gave birth to a son, Yoritomo ordered the infant killed.

Meanwhile, the dragnet tightened around Yoshitsune. Throughout the country, rewards were offered for his head. Still, he managed to elude Yoritomo for four years. Accompanied by his faithful companion, the giant Benkei, he fled north to a region not under Yoritomo's control. Yoritomo sent an army to subdue the region and at last Yoshitsune was cornered. He bade farewell to the last of his followers and killed himself. His head was sent to Kamakura in a barrel of sake, a wine made from rice.

Now master of Japan, Yoritomo made a complete break with the past. In 1192, he forced the emperor to grant him the title of *shogun*. This was a military honor that had been used in the past for warriors fighting against the emperor's enemies. But now the title carried the power to run the country in the emperor's name. For 700 years, the military would rule Japan. Moreover, the emperor's commission extended into the future. From then on, no one but a member of the Minamoto clan could be shogun.

Yoritomo chose not to rule in Kyoto because he believed that life at court would make his warrior-administrators soft and ineffective. He remained at Kamakura, which became headquarters of the military government, called the *bakufu*. The emperor, surrounded by his courtiers, stayed in Kyoto, where he continued to perform his religious duties to ensure the gods' blessings on Japan.

Yoritomo, although cruel, was a methodical and strong leader who brought order and peace to the land. He served for seven years longer until he was killed in a fall from his horse.

But the Japanese preferred the memory of Yoshitsune. The deeds and stories of the war between the Taira and the Minamoto became the material for traveling minstrels, and later, plays, puppet shows, paintings, and movies. In legend, Yoshitsune's victory and betrayal made him the great tragic hero of Japanese history. He represented, in his military valor, the ideal of the samurai.

C H A P T E R 4

"THE PILLAR OF JAPAN"—NICHIREN

At sunset on September 13, 1271, crowds of people gathered in the streets of Kamakura. They saw the shogun's guards leading a horse on which sat a man whose hands were bound. Following came the executioner with a sword. Some people looked at the prisoner with silent admiration; others jeered. The condemned man, a Buddhist monk named Nichiren, was a controversial figure with a prickly personality. He claimed to offer the only true form of Buddhism. Nichiren warned of dire consequences for Japan—foreign invasion and destruction—if it did not accept his teaching.

The bakufu government at Kamakura regarded the monk as a nuisance and a threat to the peace. For that reason it had condemned him to death. Many of his weeping followers lined the roadside to bid him farewell. As the procession wound through the streets, it passed the shrine to Hachiman, the Shinto god of war and the patron of the nation. Hachiman was so respected that in Japan he became one of the Buddhist gods as well.

Nichiren shouted a bold challenge to the god, demanding that Hachiman save him:

> When I, Nichiren, this night shall have been beheaded and shall have passed away to the Paradise of Vulture Peak, I shall declare unto Our Lord Shakyamuni [Buddha] that Thou, Hachiman, and the Sun Goddess have not fulfilled the vows. Therefore, if Thou fearest, tarry not, but do Thy duty!

The group wended its way across a wooden bridge to the small island of Enoshima, where the execution was scheduled to take place. By now it was the dead of night. A disciple of Nichiren described what happened:

> Nichiren, reciting the Scripture tirelessly, knelt down on the straw mat and bared his neck to receive the fatal stroke. Just as the executioner raised his sword, a sudden clap of thunder

shook the ground, the sky lit up, and from the black clouds fell a ball of fire which broke the lifted sword into three pieces, paralyzing the executioner's arm, and he fell to the ground.

The watching crowd began to shout for Nichiren's release. Shaken by what had happened, the guards agreed that they should check with the government before they proceeded. While on the way back to Kamakura, they met officials who were bringing a stay of execution. Word of these miraculous events spread rapidly. Many of Nichiren's followers, and the man himself, pointed to them as evidence of the truth of Nichiren's teaching.

Nichiren was born in 1222, in a small village on the Sea of Japan. Named Zennichimaro at birth, he came from humble surroundings, his father being a poor fisherman. When he was 12 years old, his father took him to a Buddhist monastery of the Tendai sect. At 15, he took holy orders and became a monk. But the young man was not completely satisfied with the life he led there, and departed. For the next 13 years he traveled in search of the true form of Buddhism.

When Buddhism came to Japan, there were already many sects within the religion. The most traditional emphasized the insignificance of worldly things. Japan accepted all the Buddhist sects with eagerness. However, Japanese Buddhism tended to emphasize the rituals and outward forms of the religion, and appealed more strongly to the nobility than to the common people. The wandering young monk sought a doctrine of salvation that would have wide appeal.

At Kamakura, the shogun's capital, he observed a new school of Buddhism that had come from China. It had gained a large following because it offered salvation to all and did not require a lifetime of study. This was the Pure Land Sect.

As Buddhism spread through Asia, its devotees recognized many other models of perfection besides the historical Buddha (Siddhartha Gautama, who had founded the religion in India). Some groups believed in a Buddha of the Future; others, in a Buddha Amida, who dwelled in the Western Paradise, or "Pure Land." All people could attain bliss and eternal life in the Pure Land. All that was necessary was to repeat the Buddha Amida's name (the Nembetsu) before their deaths.

Nichiren studied with a master of the Pure Land Sect. However, he decided this faith did not provide the answer he was seeking. He went on to Kyoto to study Zen, another Buddhist sect imported from China. The followers of Zen sought enlightenment, or *satori*, through meditation. Zen Buddhists did without sacred texts and claimed that tasks in everyday life were just as important as religious duties in reaching enlightenment. Again, Nichiren was not satisfied.

As he continued to wander and study, he developed his own ideas. In 1253, he returned to his home monastery. For seven days he stayed in seclusion before presenting himself to his fellow monks in the great hall of the temple. There he declared that all truth lay within the Lotus Sutra, one of the many respected texts of Buddhism. All other religious teachings, he proclaimed, were wrong; indeed, the Tendai rituals practiced within these very walls were useless. His declaration shocked the monks—so much so that they expelled him from the community.

Undaunted, the wandering monk took a new name for himself, Nichiren, to proclaim his mission. *Nichi*, which means "the sun," also stood for the light of truth, the rising sun that is the symbol of Japan. *Ren* means "lotus," a flower with deep symbolic meaning for Buddhists, for its pure white blossom rises from filthy muck. The lotus was also part of the Lotus Sutra, the Buddhist scripture that Nichiren believed was supreme.

Returning to Kamakura he began to preach the benefits of the Lotus Sutra. The Lotus Sutra teaches that potential Buddhahood is a possibility for all living things. All people have the Buddha within them. But the Lotus Sutra is a document that requires deep study, and Nichiren believed that it was unrealistic to expect people to take the time to understand it. However, it was such a marvelous and miraculous doctrine that its very name had power. People could earn merit just by repeating *Namu-myoho-renge-kyo* ("Homage to the Lotus Sutra.")

Nichiren had no monastery; he preached his doctrine on street corners. No part of the city was too humble for him. He offered Buddhahood to all his followers. They could attain paradise right here on earth, if they realized that Buddhahood lay within themselves. Anything was possible for people devoted to the Lotus Sutra. He preached:

If you desire to attain Buddhahood immediately, lay down the banner of pride, cast away the club of resentment, and trust yourselves to the unique Truth....Devote yourself wholeheartedly to the "Adoration to the Lotus of the Perfect Truth," and utter to yourself as well as admonish others to do the same. Such is the task in this human life.

His preaching attracted many followers. But Nichiren also openly attacked the other schools of Buddhism, often in harsh terms. In recent years, Japan had suffered from earthquakes, epidemics, and floods. Nichiren blamed these on the preaching of other sects. He claimed that all these calamities had been foretold in the scriptures and happened because Japan had abandoned the Lotus Sutra. He denounced Zen as "a doctrine of fiends and devils." But he saved particular scorn for the Pure Land Sect, blaming it for ruining the country.

Nichiren's combative style won him many enemies. Pure Land followers burned down his home, and he barely escaped being killed. Because he did not spare government officials in his denunciations, he was arrested in 1261 and exiled to the Izu Peninsula.

Two years later, he was released. Returning to Kamakura, he continued his attacks. Now he added dire predictions for Japan—internal unrest and foreign invasion. When Mongol ambassadors arrived in 1268 to demand that Japan submit to the domain of the Mongol empire, Nichiren claimed that he had foretold it. His teachings became more popular.

The fierce Mongol warriors had swept out of their homeland in Central Asia to conquer the largest land empire the world had ever seen. It stretched from the plains of Hungary in Europe to China. Yet the Japanese refused to yield to the Mongol ambassadors' demands. When a second delegation arrived, the Japanese beheaded them, bringing the tart commentary from Nichiren, "It is a great pity that they should have cut off the heads of the innocent Mongols and left unharmed the priests [of other sects], who are the enemies of Japan." He demanded that Japan adopt his religion and suppress the others. The government responded by condemning him to death, but the miraculous thunderbolt saved him.

After his close call, he was exiled to the island of Sado. While there, Nichiren worked to convert the inhabitants. His conviction that he was Japan's savior only increased. He proclaimed:

I shall be the pillar of Japan! I shall be the eyes of Japan! I shall be the well-spring of Japan! Just as now my mercy is vast and all-embracing, so will the adoration of the Lotus of Perfect Truth prevail in the ten thousand years to come, that is, time without end. This is the merit I have acquired, which is destined to open the blind eyes of all who dwell in Japan, and to close the way to the deepest of hells.

When the government learned that the Mongols were planning an invasion, it nervously released Nichiren. The year was 1274. Nichiren foretold that the time of punishment was near. Japan's last chance was to adopt the Lotus Sutra. After delivering this message, he retired to a life of contemplation in the foothills of Mount Minobu.

Within months, the Mongols landed on the coast of Kyushu. The Japanese were unaccustomed to the Mongols' style of fighting. In wars among themselves, the Japanese usually fought in single combat, with one warrior challenging another by stating his clan and achievements. The Mongols, on the other hand, overwhelmed their enemies by attacking in closely packed formations guided by gongs and drums. Moreover they had weapons the Japanese had never seen, including a kind of firebomb launched by a catapult. Still the Japanese resisted bravely and storms caused the Mongol fleet to retreat back to China.

The Mongols returned in 1281 with an even larger force. Japan was now in mortal danger. In fierce fighting on the beach, its samurai beat off the first wave of Mongol warriors. But as more and more invaders landed, it seemed unlikely that the Japanese could hold them all at bay.

As the battle raged, the emperor asked for divine intervention. All the Buddhist monasteries were asked to offer prayers for victory. The emperor sent a messenger to the shrine of Ise to ask the Sun Goddess to protect her islands.

Rarely have the effects of prayer been so dramatic. That day, the sky blackened and the sun disappeared. A typhoon swept through the waters off the Japanese coast for two days. As the storm raged, it destroyed much of the Mongol fleet. The Mongol soldiers who had already landed were hunted down and killed. The Japanese called the typhoon *kamikaze*, or "divine wind," because it clearly was the work of the gods. The victory strengthened the Japanese belief that their land was indeed under divine protection.

Nichiren took credit for the kamikaze in the few months left of his life. He died in 1282. Nevertheless, his followers kept his ideas alive. His beliefs remained popular with the humble people to whom he had preached. They also appealed to the samurai because of his strong emphasis on the importance of Japan.

Nichiren Buddhism is the only form of the religion that has developed within Japan. But Nichiren believed it had universal appeal, claiming that his religion would one day make Japan the center of a worldwide church. Indeed, an international branch of his religion, the Sokka Gokai, today has followers all over the world.

CHAPTER 5

THE TEA MASTER—SEN NO RIKYU

In the late summer of 1587, posters went up throughout Kyoto. The *kampaku*, or military head of Japan, Toyotomi Hideyoshi, was inviting the whole city to a tea party in the groves of the Kitano shrine. Hideyoshi was a great war leader who had been ruling Japan for two years. Now he was holding the party to celebrate his conquest of the island of Kyushu. The posters promised that Hideyoshi's famous tea utensils would be on display.

The "come one, come all" invitation was unusual for Japan, where the different social classes rarely mingled. But for this occasion, everyone was encouraged to bring "one kettle, one bucket, one drinking bowl" and a straw *tatami* mat to sit on. The posters promised that one of the hosts of the party would be Sen no Rikyu. Everyone knew that this man was the greatest living authority on the *chanoyu*, or tea ceremony.

The day dawned brightly. From Kyoto and beyond, warriors, merchants, and peasants came with their tea utensils. Even the *namban*, or "southern barbarians"—those strange people from a place called Europe—arrived for the party. The crowd filed into the groves of the shrine, where hundreds of temporary tea huts had been set up. As the guests arrived, they were invited to register their names at a lottery booth: the winners would be served by the kampaku himself. During the morning, he served tea to 803 people and visited with honored guests in the afternoon.

Hideyoshi hoped the event would demonstrate his refinement and culture. For that reason, having Sen no Rikyu serve as a host was an added triumph. In truth, this "Great Kitano Tea Gathering" (the largest ever held) was not the style of Sen no Rikyu. A proper tea ceremony usually was conducted in quiet, intimate surroundings. Still, the spirit of the gathering reflected his philosophy of tea. Sen no Rikyu believed that the tea ceremony offered spiritual and artistic benefits for all people.

The future tea master was born in 1522 in the port city of Sakai as Tanaka Yoshiro. The Tanaka family were prosperous merchants who ran a wholesale fishing business and operated warehouses. Sakai was one of the richest and most powerful cities in Japan at this time because it was the center of trade with China.

During the years of Yoshiro's youth, Japan suffered from constant warfare. In the words of a Japanese saying, it was a time when "The strong eat and the weak become the meat." The shogun had lost much of his power. Over time, powerful *daimyos* ("lords") had captured large areas of Japan. Most cities and towns were under the control of daimyos or of monasteries with their own fighting monks. As one samurai put it, "Only muscle counts."

The city of Sakai, however, was an exception. It enjoyed a unique degree of freedom, ruled by a citizen's council that organized the city's own military protection. The riches of the city's commerce went into culture, and no luxury was as desired as tea utensils. These included iron kettles, fine tea bowls, whisks to mix the tea with water, and tea caddies.

From a young age, Yoshiro was drawn more to culture than to business. His grandfather Sen'ami had served the shogun as official cultural advisor. In honor of his grandfather's career and to show his own goal in life, the young Yoshiro took the name Sen. Later he would receive the title Rikyu by which he is known.

Sen no Rikyu entered a Zen monastery where he discovered the world of tea. Zen monks originally drank tea for health and to keep awake during long meditation sessions. The strong tea was fermented and pressed into cakes. To make the drink, the cakes were scraped and the powder was boiled in water to make a thick broth. The broth was served in bowls. The monks found that tea-drinking had spiritual benefits as well. It produced an atmosphere of peace and a sense of community.

Over time, the utensils used for making and serving tea became regarded with the same reverence as Buddhist ritual objects. Skilled artisans made lovely iron kettles, fine pottery jars, silk or cotton containers for the tea cakes, bamboo scoops, and tea bowls. The method of preparing and serving tea became a ritual ceremony that was carried out in a small hut.

Young Rikyu studied "the way of tea" with different masters. All the motions of brewing and serving the tea had to be performed

with smooth calmness, for the ceremony had to reflect inner peace. Creating the proper atmosphere in the tea hut and using appropriate utensils were important.

Rikyu developed his own style. His four basic principles were harmony, reverence, purity, and tranquillity. The tea ceremony should put the guests in harmony with nature. Guests and host showed reverence or respect in sharing their experience. Purity was expressed by the absolute cleanliness of the tea hut and all the utensils. Tranquillity and inner peace resulted from a smooth performance of the ceremony.

Previously, the tea ceremony had been a pastime for the upper classes, who liked to display their fancy Chinese porcelain tea sets. Rikyu favored rough, plain, Japanese ceramic bowls as reminders of nature. He also did away with customs that tended to emphasize social differences. For example, it was usual to provide a basin of water so that people entering the tea room could rinse their hands and mouth. The basin was set where a noble would not have to bend over to reach it, and risk soiling his kimono. Rikyu introduced the lower basin, so that the guests had to crouch to wash, bringing everyone down to the same level.

Similarly, teahouses used to have two entrances. Servants and those of lesser birth had to crouch to get through a small door. The lord himself came in by another entrance, where he did not have to stoop. But in Sen no Rikyu's ceremonies, a small entrance was used by all. All the guests shared the humbling experience of crawling through the doorway and thus became equals no matter what their social class outside. Rikyu believed that the world of tea stood completely apart from the outside world. Even the most powerful samurai had to leave his sword outside. The tradition continues today, when briefcases, jewels, and wristwatches are discarded before entering the hut.

Rikyu's fame grew in Sakai and beyond. He attracted the attention of Oda Nobunaga, the most powerful daimyo in the land. Nobunaga was striving to unite the country under his rule. In 1568 he captured Kyoto and five years later deposed the shogun. But because Nobunaga was not a member of the Minamoto clan, he could not take that title himself. Also, many of the daimyo continued to resist him.

Nobunaga looked with eager eyes at the rich city of Sakai and soon brought it under his control. The city became an important source for his war supplies. European traders and missionaries, mostly Portuguese, had a base there, and among the goods they offered were muskets. Nobunaga quickly saw the value of these weapons in his struggle against other daimyo. He liked the Europeans he met and often dressed in western clothing.

Nobunaga also became interested in tea. He was an avid collector of utensils, and presented tea bowls to his favorite generals as rewards for their bravery and success. Seeking to add to his own collection, he sent one of his best generals, Toyotomi Hideyoshi, to Sakai. Naturally, Hideyoshi consulted Sen no Rikyu for advice and they struck up a friendship.

In 1582, Rikyu held a tea ceremony for Nobunaga at a temple in Kyoto. For the occasion, Nobunaga had brought his most valuable tea utensils from Azuchi Castle, his massive fortified headquarters. The occasion had been serene. But before the next day dawned, Nobunaga was dead, killed treacherously by a supposed ally. Both Nobunaga and his precious tea utensils were destroyed in the flames that consumed the temple.

The assassin soon met his own death at the hands of Toyotomi Hideyoshi, who now took command of Nobunaga's forces. A contemporary said of Hideyoshi, "He resembled a wizened monkey, but on the field of battle he was a veritable war-god." Hideyoshi was an unlikely leader, for he came from a peasant family—the only ruler in Japanese history to rise from the lower classes. But the fifteenth century was a period of great social movement and change. The constant warfare made the skills of a soldier more important than noble birth. The emperor granted Hideyoshi the title of *kampaku*, which had been held in early times by the Fujiwara.

Despite his power Hideyoshi was sensitive about his humble origins and craved acceptance. He was a true social climber, always trying to increase his status. As a sign of his superior culture, he appointed Rikyu as his tea master and cultural advisor. He also used Rikyu to conduct diplomatic negotiations. In the Japan of that time—and even today—it was customary to reach important decisions in intimate surroundings. In the sixteenth century, it was a tea hut; today's Japanese businessmen frequently discuss affairs in an elegant restaurant.

The relationship between the two men was sometimes stormy.

They had contrasting personalities—Hideyoshi was exuberant and liked grand gestures; Rikyu was self-assured and disciplined. But it was clear that Rikyu had influence with the kampaku. After a daimyo visited Hideyoshi, he wrote that to get to the kampaku one had to have the ear of Rikyu. A strong bond seemed to draw these opposites together.

Hideyoshi was a man of many moods and tempers. Those who dealt with him had to be careful. Once, he became offended by a slight error by his host during a tea ceremony. Hideyoshi cut off the man's nose and exiled him. But Sen no Rikyu seemed to have no fear of his master's hot temper, as the following story shows.

While a youth, Rikyu became fond of a European flower—the morning glory. He had a garden full of them. When Hideyoshi heard about it, he asked to come to take tea with the master and see these new flowers at their best. On the day when Hideyoshi arrived, he found that all the flowers in Rikyu's garden had been plucked. He proceeded to the tea hut in a foul mood. There he saw a single morning glory wet with dew, displayed in the alcove, or *tokonoma*, of the tea room. Sen no Rikyu was teaching him a lesson—"less is more." The flower's beauty could best be appreciated by focusing on a single blossom. That gives one the essence of the flower.

The friendship between the two increased when Rikyu assisted Hideyoshi in hosting a tea ceremony for the emperor himself. Hideyoshi's personal prestige had reached its high point.

Of course, he would have not had the prestige without his brilliant military successes as well. Hideyoshi continued the process of unifying Japan that Nobunaga had begun. After his conquest of Kyushu (celebrated at the Great Kitano Tea Gathering), he began a new campaign against the only daimyo who still resisted his warriors. In 1590 he conquered the last of his enemies and brought Japan under his control. Sen no Rikyu celebrated the victory with Hideyoshi.

Nevertheless, the two men came to a parting of the ways in less than a year. For some unknown reason, Hideyoshi ordered Rikyu placed under house arrest. Friends and students begged Rikyu to send his wife and son to seek mercy from the kampaku. But the tea master refused. Hideyoshi's only concession to their former friendship was to allow Rikyu to die by his own hand.

Rikyu invited his closest friends to a last tea ceremony. One by one, they made their way up the wooded path where the tea hut stood. Incense wafted from the doorway, and they stooped to crawl inside. They found a kettle of water boiling on a charcoal brazier. Finally, the host made his appearance. With steady, calm hands he made the tea and served each guest. They sat drinking in silence, with the host finishing his bowl last, by custom. Proper etiquette demanded that the guests now comment on the beauty of the tea utensils. As they did, Rikyu made a present of each item in the set to his friends. He kept only his own bowl. "Never again," he said, "shall this cup, polluted by the lips of misfortune, be used by man." He smashed the bowl into fragments.

The friends made their farewells. Rikyu removed his kimono, revealing a white death robe underneath. Drawing a dagger, he murmured a Buddhist prayer and thrust it into his body. The year was 1591.

Sen no Rikyu is a very important figure in Japanese cultural history. The tea ceremony has affected such Japanese arts as flower arranging, gardens, and ceramics. Moreover, the ideals of the tea ceremony—cleanliness, simplicity, naturalness, and a sense of proportion—express the deepest values of the Japanese on human conduct and nature. The ceremony remains today a living part of Japanese life and culture.

C H A P T E R   6

A Free Spirit—Okuni

On an April day in 1603, a crowd of people gathered on the banks of the Kamo River in Kyoto. At this time of year, the river bed was dry, and word had spread that a woman was using it as a stage. The throng of samurai, merchants, commoners, and some Portuguese waited eagerly for the performance to begin.

Soon the performer called Okuni appeared. Her black hair was cut short like a man's. She wore a crimson robe covered with gold embroidery and tied at the waist with a purple sash. As she began to dance, a golden rosary swung around her neck and two gold-plated swords jangled at her side. To the sound of drums, bells, and gongs she glided across the dry earth, her arms and legs flowing with the music. The onlookers were fascinated.

The other young women in her troupe joined Okuni. They began to perform little skits in pantomime. Wordlessly, simply by changing her expression and the way she held her body, Okuni became a strutting samurai, then turned into a seductive young woman. The spectators laughed at her antics, and then nudged each other as the performance took a sexy turn. To lively music, the dancers gaily imitated drunken revelers. Then the music slowed and Okuni crumpled to the ground like a lover who had killed herself. Revived by the others, she began a new skit.

At the finish, the applause of the audience echoed along the riverbank. A star was born, and with her a brand-new form of musical drama in Japan. Okuni's troupe soon was drawing enormous crowds to the riverside. The people of Kyoto coined a new word for her performances—*kabuki*. It meant something that was daring and unconventional. It carried the idea of stepping beyond the bounds of what was proper. Okuni herself was a free spirit who never let herself be bound by tradition.

Okuni was born around 1571. Her father, Komura Sanemon,

was a blacksmith for the Izumo Shrine, one of the holiest Shinto religious sites. It was dedicated to a descendant of the kami Susanoo, who, according to legend, had settled at Izumo after being exiled from heaven. Okuni grew up here and became an attendant at the central Izumo Shrine, home of the kami who blesses marriage.

As part of her duties, she learned the sacred Shinto dance, the *kagura*. The kagura included mime performances that were intended to make the kami, and the spectators, laugh. By custom, the dancers sometimes performed in the local community to raise money for the shrine. As a girl, Okuni accompanied priests and priestesses on such missions. Her performances attracted attention. Though she is said not to have been particularly beautiful, an inner spark of talent marked her as someone special. She soon became a minor celebrity, in demand beyond the confines of Izumo.

Her first recorded public appearance took place at Kyoto in 1586, when she was 15. She began with a prayer-dance, carrying a bell that she rang to accompany her movements. It was not long before the wealthy and powerful summoned her to appear before them. Supposedly she performed for Hideyoshi himself.

The priests at Izumo Shrine were displeased by Okuni's growing fame. They demanded that she return to her place as a priestess for the gods. But the lure of the dancer's life was more attractive, and she refused. Furthermore, she took some of the shrine's most talented performers with her. In retaliation, Okuni's father and family were expelled from the shrine.

Okuni started to develop her art further, going beyond the ritual dances she had learned. Adding words, she began to perform short skits. She incorporated Buddhist dances and some elements of the *No* plays, which had been created 200 years before. *No* drama was a highly rigid art form, popular among the nobility. It used a small number of actors, usually only two, who moved in slow, highly stylized movements. But *No* actors wore masks, which Okuni's troupe did not. She added fantastic costumes and spiced her skits with racy humor and sex. As a twist, she performed male roles and used male actors for female roles.

Among the stories Okuni drew on for inspiration was the saga of the brothers Yoshitsune and Yoritomo. Okuni took the tragic tale and brought it to life on the stage with music and dance. Her favorite episode, not surprisingly, was the dance of Shizuka.

Okuni often concluded her performances with a general dance, inviting the audience to join in. These merry, sometimes riotous, scenes attracted the *kabukimono*, the nonconformists of their time. They were rebelling against the rigid society that had resulted from the rise to power of Tokugawa Ieyasu.

Ieyasu was the last of the three great warriors who unified Japan after a century of civil war. He was a daimyo who had been one of the first to form an alliance with Nobunaga. After Nobunaga's death, Ieyasu had reluctantly accepted the leadership of Hideyoshi. When Hideyoshi died in 1598, Ieyasu made his move to pick up the reins of power. Two years later at the Battle of Sekigahara, the Tokugawa forces were victorious and the emperor granted Ieyasu the title of shogun. He made his capital at Edo (today's Tokyo). Under Ieyasu and his descendants, the Tokugawa shogunate would rule Japan till 1868.

Now that Ieyasu held unchallenged power, he took steps to create a Japan that would remain orderly. One of his goals was to stamp out European influences.

Fads for European things had become popular. Japanese artists painted *namban* screens that showed the Europeans in their outlandish dress. It was not uncommon for a samurai to have a cross engraved on his saddle just to be up-to-date. Tobacco and some western foods such as sponge cake and *tempura* (food dipped in batter and fried) became part of Japanese life.

A European described the Japanese love for European "styles" in a letter:

They wear rosaries of driftwood on their breasts, hang a cruci-
fix from their shoulder or waist, and sometimes even a hand-
kerchief. Some who are especially kindly disposed, have
memorized the Our Father and the Hail Mary, and recite them
as they walk in the streets. This is not done in ridicule of the
Christians, but simply to show off their familiarity with the lat-
est fashion. This has led them to spend no small sums in order-
ing oval earrings bearing the likeness of Our Lord and the Holy
Mother.

The kabukimono, like Okuni herself, were among those who
took up Christian symbols as a sign of their modern ways. They felt
at odds with Tokugawa Ieyasu's attempt to restore order to Japanese society. Okuni was their natural heroine, for her art scoffed at
authority. After her 1603 performance in the riverbed, kabuki
dances became the rage. Many kabukimono themselves took to the
stage, singing what we might translate today as, "Now let's get
funky....Come on, be funky."

Tokugawa Ieyasu was not pleased with the reports about
kabuki and the dangerous sentiments that it aroused. It was said
that young kabukimono insulted merchants' wives and challenged
people to duels over trivial matters. But the shogun's second son
was enchanted with Okuni's art. After a performance he exclaimed,
"Of all among the tens of millions of women in the world, does she
[Okuni] not stand alone?"

Okuni probably died around 1610. There is no mention of her
in the records after this. The women who followed her lacked her
talent and the shows became quite daring. Shockingly, court ladies
copied the styles of kabuki actresses, and men fought for the actresses' favors. A Japanese wrote that men who pursued the actresses
"...threw away their wealth, some forgot their fathers and mothers,
others did not care if the mothers of their children were jealous."

In 1629, the shogun banned women from the kabuki stage and
restricted the performances to certain sections of the cities. Samurai
were forbidden to attend kabuki plays. Even so, kabuki could not
be stamped out. It developed into Japan's most popular form of
drama. But ironically, classical kabuki, an art founded by a woman,
today has no female actors.

"NO FANCY PRICES"— MITSUI SHUHO

In the early years of the seventeenth century, a 13-year-old girl (later known as Shuho) was brimming with hope for her future. Secretly, she left her home to go to the local Shinto shrine. She wrote the name of the man she was going to marry, Mitsui Sokubei, on paper sheets to hang on the sacred trees in the grove. She believed the sacred kami would see the name and grant her wish for a happy marriage.

A short time later, the wedding was held in the Mitsui home. By Japanese custom, the ceremony was just for the families. A Shinto priest begged the kami to bless the marriage. The bride and groom exchanged three cups of sake (rice wine), sipping each cup three times, which was the essential rite of the ceremony (as it is today).

This wedding was unusual because the bride was from a merchant family and the groom was a samurai. Under the Tokugawa shoguns, Japanese society was rigidly divided into four classes. In descending order of rank, these were: samurai, farmer, craftsworker, and merchant. Only the samurai could carry the two swords (one long, one short) that marked their rank. Farmers were second in importance because they provided food for the nation. Merchants were the lowest of all, because they lived off the work of others and did not produce anything themselves.

Most samurai scorned the lowly merchant class. But the Mitsui family had fallen on hard times, and marrying one of their sons to a merchant's daughter was a way to increase the wealth of the family. In fact, this marriage marked the beginning of a family business today known the world over.

Shuho was born around 1590. Her father was known for his generous gifts to the shrines of the area, including Ise. Shuho inher-

ited not only wealth but also an uncanny ability for business.

Her samurai husband, according to family legend, was descended from a member of the Fujiwara family who left Kyoto around 1100 to live on the shore of Lake Biwa. While looking over his new property, this ancestor discovered three wells; in one of them he found a hoard of gold coins. To mark his good fortune, he changed his name to Mitsui, which means "three wells."

Over time the Mitsui family became known as the Lords of Echigo. When Oda Nobunaga started to unite Japan, he swept into the Mitsui lands, looting and destroying. But the Mitsuis showed the prudence for which they would later be famous. Sensing the coming danger, the head of the family, Takayasu, gathered his valuables, his family, and a few retainers, and fled.

Through incredible luck he traveled safely across the wartorn country to the Ise peninsula. He settled in the peaceful town of Matsusaka, a flourishing port for the coastal trade. Pilgrims on the road to the Ise Shrine often stopped in the town, bringing news about developments in the rest of the country. The Mitsuis learned that Tokugawa Ieyasu had won the title of shogun.

Takayasu's eldest son, Sokubei, grew up to be a gentleman of leisure who liked to dabble in the arts. Sokubei needed money to pursue these interests, and was perfectly content to marry the daughter of a merchant family.

Shuho proved to be a good match for her husband. She bore him four sons and four daughters, and provided for her growing family with remarkable thriftiness. In fact, Shuho became legendary for cutting corners any way she could. The family ate very simple meals. No child could leave the table until his or her rice bowl was empty. The children wore clothes made from cotton that was grown and woven in the Ise region. The garments were handed down from child to child until they were threadbare. Even broken pottery was put to good use—Shuho filled a bottomless vat with the pieces and made it a tank to hold rainwater. A leaky wooden dipper became a flower stand. Even the straw that was used to separate sheets of writing paper was saved to absorb the oil in fried food. Shuho required each of her children, from the youngest to the eldest, to perform chores for the welfare of the family. They never forgot her lessons of the value of thrift and savings.

In 1616, Sokubei made a trip to Edo, the Tokugawa capital. It was a momentous year for both Japan and the Mitsui family. Tokugawa Ieyasu died, having put down the last challenge to his rule. The old warrior handed over to his descendants a stable government that would last until 1868. He had cut back on Japan's relations with the rest of the world, prohibiting missionaries from the country and limiting foreign trade to a trickle.

Sokubei saw that Edo was becoming a wealthy city. The city's merchants were making fortunes. Here lay the future of Japan. On his return, he called Shuho and the children together to make an important announcement. They gathered in a room that held the family shrine honoring the Mitsui ancestors. A suit of armor hung there as a reminder of his family's military past.

Sokubei bowed to the shrine and clapped his hands to attract the attention of his ancestors' spirits. He explained to them that to ensure the Mitsui family's continued prosperity, he would renounce the empty privileges of the samurai. "A great peace is at hand," he declared. "The shogun rules firmly and with justice at Edo. No more shall we have to live by the sword. I have seen that great profit can be made honorably. I shall brew sake and soy sauce, and we shall prosper." With this, Sokubei exchanged his samurai's sword for the abacus, a calculating device that was the symbol of a Japanese tradesman.

Brewing sake and making soy sauce (used in place of salt in cooking) was not difficult. The family needed only a few workers and a small amount of money. What made this family business different was that it was run by a former samurai. People came to call it *Echigo-no-sakaya*: Lord Echigo's sake shop.

Sokubei, unfortunately, turned out to have little talent for business. He had no head for figures and found selling goods less to his liking than practicing calligraphy (beautiful handwriting) or writing poetry. Few customers came into the shop. But Shuho stepped in and saved the business. She had the merchant skills that her husband lacked, as well as boundless energy and dedication.

To attract the servants of wealthy families, Shuho offered them tobacco or tea when they came shopping. She kept prices low and gave friendly and courteous service. The quality of her sake wine began to draw farmers on market days, sailors on leave, and pilgrims on their way to the Ise Shrine. Indeed, Shuho's hospitality persuaded some of them to spend more than they should.

Sometimes they had to borrow money from her to get home. She allowed them to leave their valuables as security for borrowed money. From this beginning, Shuho opened a pawnshop as a side business. The interest on the loans and the money from selling unclaimed valuables became very profitable.

But Shuho was thinking beyond Matsusaka. She had been impressed by her husband's tales of Edo. The people of Edo were known as spendthrifts. She gave her eldest son some money and sent him to the capital. He bought cloth and opened a dry goods shop that he called Echigoya after his grandfather's title. Before long, another son joined him.

In 1633 when Shuho was 43, her husband died. By that time only her youngest son, Hachirobei, was left at home. She recognized that he had the most business talent in the family, and sent him to Edo to learn from his brothers. He was so successful that he soon opened a second Echigoya. On the sign that graced the shop was a slogan that came straight from his mother's teachings: "No Fancy Prices." When he found that customers of other stores were dissatisfied because they had to buy a certain amount of cloth at a time, he offered to cut any length the customer wished. Hachirobei also kept a stock of oil-paper umbrellas to lend to customers when it rained. Because the umbrellas were decorated with the Mitsui crest, they were walking advertisements. Over time his shop would

grow into the first department store in Japan. Today, it is the most popular and fashionable store in Tokyo—the Mitsukochi.

Happy with the success of her family, Shuho kept operating the sake and soy sauce business and the pawnshop. She worked long hours, often late into the night. Her honesty and shrewdness became legendary. One morning she found in the street a purse made of striped cloth. It contained 30 *ryos*, the currency of Japan during the Tokugawa period. She sent errand boys throughout the town to find material that matched the purse. In this way she traced the owner and returned the money. People repeated the story, adding to her reputation.

Shuho turned to religion more strongly after her husband's death. She rose each morning at four o'clock and bathed in cold water. Then she repeated Buddhist prayers and prayed to Shinto kami before opening the shop. She traveled to shrines regularly. But even these pilgrimages were opportunities for Shuho's thrift. On the road, she picked up worn-out sandals and straw horseshoes, saving them to be used for fuel or compost. She even collected the strings that men and women used to hold up their hair. Taking the bits home, she wound them into big balls for use in her shop.

Shuho lived to be a very old woman, but her sons never stopped asking her shrewd advice on business decisions. When she sensed that her end was coming, she called for Hachirobei. Even though Shuho was now enormously wealthy, she had not lost her discipline and love for thrift. She told Hachirobei exactly how much money he should spend on her funeral. Then she gave a detailed accounting of how she wanted her belongings to be disposed of.

Leaving nothing to chance, she had sandbags placed on the shelf above her bed. These were to be propped against her body after death so that she could lie in a dignified manner. When all her cares had been satisfied, it is said that she murmured Buddhist prayers until she died in 1676. She was 85 years old.

From the indomitable will of this remarkable woman sprang the oldest business empire in the world. Her descendants would open shops, a bank (the oldest existing bank in the world), and become involved in every phase of Japan's economy. Today the Mitsui business empire is one of Japan's largest, including real estate, insurance, and transportation companies. It owes a debt of gratitude to Shuho, who made it all possible.

C H A P T E R 8

"Bewitched by the Travel Gods"—Basho

Around the year 1680, a popular poet left the busy city of Edo. Having become famous, he found that there were too many distractions for him to write. He longed to return to the peace of nature. A rich fish salesman who admired poetry offered a hut on his estate near the Sumida River to the east of Edo. He also provided the poet with food and clothing.

A few followers helped him move his possessions. One of them presented the poet with a Japanese banana tree or *basho*, to plant outside. The basho tree was delicate; its large, thin leaves were easily torn by the winds. It became a symbol of the poet's sensitivity to nature. Soon his home came to be called the Banana Hermitage or *Basho-an*. The poet himself took the name by which he is known today: Basho. No Japanese poet is more loved and respected than he.

Basho was born in the town of Ueno in 1644. His father was a samurai in the service of the Todo family that ruled the city. Ueno was a training center for *ninjas*, or "invisible persons," feared fighters who were used on special assignments by Japan's daimyos. They were best known as assassins who could penetrate the most heavily guarded places to strike down their enemies. Novice ninjas became highly skilled in martial arts such as judo and in the use of bizarre weapons, such as whirling discs with razor-sharp teeth.

At the age of nine, Basho, called Kinsaku as a child, became a page in the Todo household. He was a companion and study mate for the Todo heir Yoshitada, who was two years older. The boys formed a close friendship. Because Yoshitada's health was delicate, his education emphasized literary accomplishments instead of the martial arts. He and Basho learned how to write what was called

"linked verse." This was a skill expected of all cultured Japanese, and a source of amusement in social gatherings. At its simplest, a linked verse was a five-line poem called a *waka*. Two poets composed the lines in a kind of competition. One would write the first three lines; the second would complete the last two lines.

In 1666, Yoshitada died suddenly. The pain of the loss of his boyhood friend would stay with Basho throughout his life. More than 20 years later, the poet returned to Ueno in the spring. Sitting under the blooming cherry trees where he and Yoshitada had played long ago, he wrote this poem:

> Many, many things
> they bring to mind—
> Cherry blossoms!

The flowers of the cherry tree recalled not only the happiness of youth, but were poetic symbols of samurai who died while still in the bloom of youth.

At the time of his friend's death, Basho asked the Todo family to release him from their service. When they refused, he ran away to Kyoto, renouncing his samurai status. He found refuge in a monastery, studying poetry.

A lifelong wanderer, Basho soon tired of the monastic life. In 1672, he set out for Edo, the bustling center of Tokugawa power. Edo was growing by leaps and bounds and when he first arrived, Basho was dazed by the bustling activity all around him. He took a minor position at the waterworks department to tide him over.

Meanwhile he kept writing and his poems began to attract attention. In Edo reputations could be made in a short time, and soon Basho was admired as a poet and a critic. He wrote a kind of poetry called *haiku*. A haiku was simply the first three lines of the linked verse. The first line had five syllables; the second, seven; and the third, five more for a total of 17. The point of a haiku was to create a scene or emotion through these few syllables. Basho and other great writers managed to create amazingly rich and vivid poems in this seemingly simple form. Today, the haiku is Japan's most popular form of poetry. Each year, a national haiku contest is held and the winners are invited to the emperor's palace at the New Year's celebration.

The best known haiku of all is Basho's:

An ancient pond;
A frog leaps in;
The sound of water.

As you read it, can't you just hear the splash?

At the time Basho lived, Japan and Edo were in the midst of the most creative period of the Tokugawa era. The kabuki theater was flourishing, supported by the rich merchant class of the city. It had blossomed further from the time of Okuni. A younger author named Chikamatsu was writing Japan's greatest plays for both the kabuki stage and the puppet theater.

As Basho's own reputation grew, he attracted followers who wished to learn the master's art. His poems were published in books, and people recognized him in the street. The demands on his time became too great. As we have seen, he fled to a refuge away from the hurly-burly of the city.

In his simple hut, Basho turned inward. He thought more deeply about poetry and studied Zen Buddhism. Like a priest, he shaved his head and wore black robes and straw sandals. In his art, Basho sought both the eternal truth and the fresh observation. He advised his followers: "Do not seek to follow in the footsteps of the men of old; seek what they sought." He meant that they should not imitate others, but preserve their goal of producing something that was new and beautiful.

Soon Basho grew restless again. He longed to get away, writing, "Everything about me was bewitched by the travel gods, and my thoughts were no longer mine to control. The spirits of the road beckoned, and I could do no work at all." He set out on a series of journeys throughout Japan. His travel diaries, which he called "the mutterings of a man in his sleep," are among the classic works of Japanese literature. Many travelers today retrace his path with a copy of his diary in hand.

He joined the crowds on the Tokaido Road that connected Kyoto and Edo. The Tokaido was probably the busiest highway in the world at that time. A series of inns provided lodging and meals, and the shogun's guards patrolled the road to keep it free from robbers. Basho walked with other travelers, traders, and pilgrims going to the Ise Shrine. Branches led off the main road, and Basho's wandering feet took him through farm villages and lonely places where only an occasional fisherman could be seen. Even here, fame preceded him, and he was always able to find someone willing to shelter him. Aspiring poets showed him their work, which he would patiently criticize.

Basho's longest journey was undertaken in 1688 to the north of Japan. Thinking he might meet death on the way, Basho sold his hut. He had never seen this region before, and used old books to guide him. From this journey came his book, "The Narrow Road of Oku." It begins,

> The months and days are the travelers of eternity. The years that come and go are also voyagers. Those who float away their lives on boats or who grow old leading horses are forever journeying, and their homes are wherever their travels take them. Many of the men of old died on the road, and I too for years past have been stirred by the sight of a solitary cloud drifting with the wind, to ceaseless thoughts of roaming.

Basho was deeply moved when he visited the spot where Yoshitsune had committed suicide. A castle had once stood there; now there were only rice fields. He wrote, "I sat down on my hat and wept bitterly till I almost forgot time."

Afterward, he composed this haiku:

> The summer grasses—
> All that has survived from
> Brave warriors' dreams.

On his return, Basho moved into another hut near Edo, which he called "the Unreal Dwelling." He felt himself growing old, writing, "My body, now close to fifty years of age, has become an old tree that bears bitter peaches, a snail which has lost its shell, a bagworm separated from its bag; it drifts with the winds and clouds that know no destination."

Even his poetry brought little comfort. Looking back on his life, he seems to have wished he had cured himself of the habit of writing verse:

> The conflict has waged within me, and because of it I have not enjoyed peace of mind. For a time I hoped to make a successful career for myself, but I was prevented by my poetry. For a time I thought I would study Buddhism and dispel my ignorance, but this hope was also shattered by my poetry. In the end, incapable and talentless as I am, I have tied myself to this one line of work.

However, one last journey lay ahead of him. Some of his faithful followers urged him to come to Osaka. He could not resist. Perhaps it was a flash of vanity, for Osaka was the one major city where his work was not well known. But on arrival, he found himself welcomed warmly, receiving many invitations from people who wanted to see the great poet.

The round of parties in Osaka further weakened his health. On October 8th, 1694, four days before his death, a student heard sounds from the master's bedroom: "On the night of October the eighth, though it was almost midnight ...I heard the clatter of an ink bar rubbing against a slab. I wondered what manner of letter it was, but it turned out to be a poem. It was entitled 'Sick in Bed'":

> Seized with a disease
> Halfway on the road,
> My dreams keep revolving
> Round the withered moor.

It was Basho's last poem.

CHAPTER 9

"An Old Man Mad With Painting"—Hokusai

On a day in 1804, the shogun Ienari stopped in a temple while on his way to a hunting expedition. A sudden whim struck him. Recently, he had been hearing stories about a popular artist named Hokusai, who lived near the temple. The artist was supposed to be so talented that he could capture any scene or person. His works were sold as paintings, prints, even greeting cards for New Year's. Ienari just had to see this man's work. He sent a messenger to command him to appear and give a demonstration of his talents.

Cantankerous and sometimes just plain ornery, Hokusai mulled over the shogun's order. He had to go, of course. But Hokusai was a proud man, who hated to be commanded to do anything or to humble himself before even the greatest official. Still, he loved to show off his amazing skill and realized that the publicity would give him a boost in Edo's highly competitive art world.

He went to the temple where the shogun and his group of courtiers awaited. Mustering all his dignity, Hokusai strode to the center of the room, carrying a mysterious box. After unrolling a long paper on the floor, he brushed two parallel blue lines on its surface. Hokusai had painted a flowing stream. Then he opened the box and out popped a rooster. Hokusai quickly dipped the bird's feet in red ink. As the rooster strutted across the paper, it left foot prints that looked much like maple leaves.

"I have created a landscape for Your Gracious Excellency," said Hokasai, bowing low. Amid nervous laughter from the courtiers, Hokusai dubbed his painting "Red Maples Along Tatsuta River." The title referred to a famous poem that describes maple leaves floating on that river. The shogun was enchanted. When word of the event spread, new customers and pupils flocked to the artist's studio.

The future painter was born in 1760, into a poor family in the Edo neighborhood called Katsushita. From his birthplace, the artist would take his surname later in life. His given name was Tokitaro. At the age of three, Tokitaro was adopted into the home of Nakajima Ise, the mirror polisher to the shogunate. He was expected to follow his adoptive father's profession and someday inherit the business. But it was not to be. From at least the age of six, Hokusai had, in his own words, "a mania for sketching." In his early teens, he was apprenticed to a wood engraver.

Wood-block prints were a passion of the Edokko (people of Edo). They loved to look at pictures of the life of their city. From the middle of the eighteenth century, these pictures were mass-produced on hand-cut printing blocks. The most popular prints were *ukiyo-e*, which depicted the "floating world"—the pleasure district of the city where theaters, restaurants, and wrestling booths could be found. Here lived actors, storytellers, jesters, and *geishas*—women who were trained in the arts of conversation, singing, and playing musical instruments. People of all classes came here to forget their cares and enjoy a release from their everyday lives.

A Japanese described the attractions of this floating world:

> Living only for the moment, turning our full attention to the pleasures of the moon, sun, the cherry blossoms and the maple leaves, singing songs, drinking wine, and diverting ourselves just in floating, floating, caring not a whit for the pauperism staring us in the face, refusing to be disheartened, like a gourd floating along with the river current: this is what we call the floating world [ukiyo].

Working for the wood engraver, the budding artist learned to cut letters and figures. It was an exacting skill to transfer to wood the picture that an artist had drawn on paper. Later in his career, the artist would complain about the engraving done from his own sketches. "I suggest that the engraver should add no lower eyelids where I did not draw them," he wrote in an angry letter. But for now, the work fired the youngster's ambition to become a woodcut artist himself. At 18, he was accepted as a pupil by Katsukawa Shunsho, one of the most popular printmakers of the day.

Shunsho immediately recognized the boy's great talent. He became the master's star pupil, and took Shunro as his artistic name. It was a common practice to take a name with the same syllables as the master's. During this time, the young man made prints of famous Edo beauties, sumo wrestlers, landscapes, birds, and flowers. He proved particularly adept at illustrating the novelettes that were eagerly read by the Edokko—usually spicy tales about the city. Shunsho was a lenient master and allowed his talented pupil to experiment quite freely.

After Shunsho's death, however, the young man found it difficult to get along with the other pupils. They were determined to carry on the master's memory by imitating his style, and were horrified by Shunro's determination to work as he pleased. Shunro cared little what they thought. He often quarreled with them. Soon, he was dismissed from the school and lost the right to keep his name. Throughout his career, Hokusai would use more than 30 artistic names. Whenever he changed his style, he would change his name. If he felt a change in his life, a new name reflected that too. Not until he was 38 did he take the name Hokusai, which is the name by which history knows him.

Hokusai launched his own independent career. It was astonishing both for its length and productivity—he created more than 40,000 works of all kinds over a seven-decade-long career. There were many reasons for his success. First, Hokusai, a man of great vitality, studied his art and craft throughout his life. Second, he worked hard. Despite his eccentricities and showing off, he always became serious when it came to his art. But the most amazing aspect of Hokusai was his enormous curiosity about everything. Nothing escaped his eye; no scene was too trivial to escape his brush. It was said he "lived with brush in his hand."

The great range of Hokusai's work can be seen in the sketchbooks that his pupils and friends encouraged him to publish. He called these sketches *manga*, which means "irresponsible pictures." This 15-volume work has a little of everything: monsters, animals, birds, fat people, thin people, noodle sellers, castles, weapons, magic tricks, ghosts, and imaginary creatures. Like Leonardo da Vinci, Hokusai sketched incessantly and had a consuming interest in the way things work.

He often made fun of people's faults. For example, he drew three grotesque men trying to climb tall eels near the signboard of an eel restaurant. It was a visual joke illustrating the Edo slang term "eel climb"—the struggle that ambitious people went through to prosper in business or raise their social status. Hokusai's sketches were the forerunners of the Japanese comic books (also called manga) that are wildly popular with both children and adults in Japan today.

In his personal life, Hokusai was a true eccentric. Although he was a successful artist, he was often out of cash, for he really didn't seem to care about money. He kept a large wastebasket near the entrance of his shop. When a customer came to pay for his art, he was told to drop the money in the wastebasket. When bill collectors arrived, Hokusai told them to look in the basket. As a result he lived in poverty and dressed in rags.

Hokusai was always on the move, living in more than 90 homes during his career. Sometimes he moved when his rooms got too dirty to clean up. Other times, he was one step ahead of a landlord insisting on being paid rent. When he was completely broke, he had to hide, and he became known as "the gentleman who lives in such and such a place."

Hokusai had the instincts of a showman. He loved to show off his versatility. He sometimes painted with the legs of stools, and even tore off his own clothes to use as brushes. In 1804, he gave a famous demonstration of painting to a crowd at a temple in Edo.

CHAPTER 10

THE LAST SAMURAI—
SAIGO TAKEMORI

Rain fell as morning dawned on May 15, 1868. Near Ueno Hill in northeast Edo, Lake Shinobazu overflowed, turning the surrounding roads to mud. In the drizzle, two forces of soldiers faced each other. One, commanded by Saigo Takemori, fought under the banner of the emperor. The other soldiers were die-hard followers of the Tokugawa shogun. Throughout the day, the troops of both sides fought savagely in the wet and blustery weather.

The battle was the climax of 15 years of upheaval in Japan. For over 250 years, the country had known peace and stability. The Tokugawa shoguns had run the government from their castle in Edo, while the emperors reigned in Kyoto—with no political power, performing only their religious duties. But in 1853, black steamships from the United States had arrived off the coast, ending Japan's long isolation from the outside world.

Commodore Matthew Perry, the leader of the American fleet, had demonstrated the firepower of his ships' cannons. He requested that Japan open its ports to trade. Later he showed the Japanese models of modern inventions such as locomotives and telegraphs. Impressed by this show of power, the shogun had yielded to the demands of the United States government.

The shogun's weakness in dealing with the Americans destroyed the Tokugawa regime. As European nations began to seek similar trade concessions, many Japanese feared that their country would be humiliated. Japanese patriots turned to the emperor to preserve Japan's ancient traditions. Their rallying cry was "Revere the emperor, expel the barbarians." The shogun, caught between two forces that he could not control, resigned and turned over Edo Castle to the emperor's forces. It was the end of 700 years of military rule that had begun with Minamoto Yoritomo.

Even so, some of the shogun's retainers refused to accept the loss of their power. The diehards made a base in a temple on Ueno Hill where the shoguns worshiped. They fortified it with a small cannon, and draped straw tatami mats over the walls.

General Saigo arrived with his forces to destroy the last resistance to the emperor's new power. He moved his own cannons to the second story of a nearby restaurant, and opened fire on the rebel fortress. After silencing its gun, Saigo's forces began a headlong assault. They smashed their way into the temple, where the samurai of both sides fought desperate battles with their swords.

By nightfall, the temple was on fire and the shogun's supporters were annihilated. General Saigo was the hero of the nation.

Saigo Takemori was born in 1827, the oldest of seven children of a samurai family. His birthplace was Satsuma province on the island of Kyushu. Saigo's father was a retainer for the lord of Shimazu. Founded by a relative of Minamoto Yoritomo, the Shimazu family had ruled the province for 700 years.

Young Saigo was a powerful, fearless young man who loved physical challenges. He put his weight to good use as a sumo wrestler. At school, his magnetic personality made him the leader of the other boys of samurai rank. Also mischievous, he led the others in pranks. Among his closest school friends was Okubo Toshimichi, who would play an important role in his life.

Proud of his heritage, young Saigo was devoted to the samurai code of honor, known as *bushido* or "way of the warrior." The first value of bushido was that the samurai owed his loyalty and life to his daimyo or lord. The samurai must never forget *jiri*, or duty. He must be willing to make any sacrifice to fulfill his duty—either to his daimyo or to any other person to whom he pledged his word. Once he undertook a duty, not even death should stand in his way. Accepting death as part of duty, the samurai did not fear it. Indeed, he preferred it to defeat. As one of the classic books on bushido states, "The way of the samurai is found in death."

Saigo became a retainer of Shimazu Nariakira, the lord of Satsuma. Nariakira was a progressive man who wished to modernize and reform his domain. Saigo won his friendship and trust. The lord of Satsuma was hostile to the shogun and used Saigo as a confidential agent in his intrigues against the government. Saigo car-

ried secret messages to the emperor's courtiers who opposed the shogun's cowardly dealings with the Western traders. During this time, Saigo befriended a priest in Kyoto, named Gessho, who also supported the anti-shogun movement.

When Nariakira died suddenly, Saigo was deeply grieved. To show loyalty to his lord, he resolved to commit suicide, a practice called *junshi*. Gessho, who had aroused the suspicion of the shogun's spies, resolved to join him. Together, they escaped to Satsuma to carry out their plan. One evening, telling friends they were going to admire the moon, they rowed a boat into Kagoshima Bay. Exchanging farewells, each of them wrote death poems before jumping overboard. But the splash attracted attention, and rescuers fished two bodies out of the water. Gessho was dead. Saigo lived. He was then 30 years old.

This event haunted Saigo for the rest of his life. He often expressed regret that he had failed in his duty. Each year, he marked the anniversary of his friend's drowning. For the tenth anniversary, he dedicated a poem to Gessho's spirit:

> Clasped in each other's arms we leapt into the abyss of the sea.
> Though we both jumped together, Fate foiled my expectations
>   and brought me back alive above the waves.
> Now more than ten years have followed like a trail of dreams

And I stand here before your grave, separated by death's great
  wall,
While my tears still flow in vain.

The new lord of Satsuma exiled Saigo, sending him as a prisoner to a small island. Ever true to the samurai ideal of jiri, Saigo
calmly entered the cage that had been built to transport him. When
his guard offered to release him from the cage once they were at
sea, Saigo responded: "Thank you, but whatever happens, I have to
obey the Lord [of Satsuma]. I am a convict, and I must be where a
convict should be."

For five years, Saigo remained in exile. During that time,
Japan's weakness became even more obvious. British warships
bombarded the city of Kagoshima after a British citizen had been
killed in a street fight with a Satsuma clansman. The proud
Satsuma had no military answer to the superior technology. It was
clear that Japan had to move forward quickly to avoid further
Western intrusion. Saigo's old friend Okubo went to the lord of
Satsuma and threatened to commit suicide if Saigo was not
released. The daimyo gave in.

In 1864, Saigo returned to Satsuma. By now opposition to the
shogun was widespread. Saigo tried to win the support of other
clans in a restoration of the emperor. But fighting broke out between
the Satsuma and their traditional enemies the Choshu clan. Saigo
led the Satsuma forces to victory, but afterward he spared the lives
of the Choshu prisoners. (Traditionally, they would have been exe-
cuted or forced to kill themselves.) Saigo's clemency helped him to
make the Choshu clan an ally. He forged a military alliance, and led
the imperial forces to victory against the last supporters of the
shogun in 1868.

The formation of a new government with the emperor at its
head is called the Meiji Restoration because it happened during the
reign of the Meiji emperor. The emperor moved to Edo, which was
renamed Tokyo ("eastern capital"), and the shogun's castle became
the Imperial Palace as it still is today. Among the samurai, loyalty
to the emperor took the place of loyalty to the daimyo.

But the 12-year-old emperor did not really rule. Young samurai became officials of the new government and gave orders in his
name. Their attitude toward the outside world changed; the cry to
"expel the barbarians" was set aside. The Meiji officials realized

that for Japan to become a strong country, it had to learn from the West—just as it had once learned from China.

Though Saigo's friends urged him to participate in the new government, he chose to return to Satsuma. But a delegation of officials, led by his school friend Okubo, came to beg him to serve. Against his better judgment Saigo answered his country's call.

His new mission was to create something new for Japan—a modern army composed of ordinary citizens. He trained the first recruits personally and was given the title of field marshal. But the changes in Japan challenged everything Saigo cherished. Over time, the government revoked the traditional privileges of the samurai, such as the right to wear their hair in a distinctive topknot and finally even the right to wear the two swords.

Japan rushed to adopt Western technology and develop its own modern industries. In time, the emperor's officials embraced all the trappings of Western civilization—even wearing silk top hats and frock coats. Saigo felt like a fish out of water. He dressed in a plain robe bearing the Satsuma crest and wore straw sandals on his enormous feet. One night while leaving the palace grounds during a rainstorm, he removed his sandals and walked barefoot. A suspicious palace guard stopped him. Saigo was questioned until an official driving past in his carriage told the guard that he was holding the field marshal of Japan.

Saigo avoided the western-style banquets of government officials, preferring to share noodles and simple Japanese food with his secretary and retainers. While other government officials built mansions for themselves, he rented a modest home in Tokyo. He clung to his samurai ideals, writing prophetically: "A man of true sincerity will be an example to the world even after his death...."

It was a source of sadness to him that his friend Okubo had apparently forgotten these teachings. Once, when Saigo learned that Okubo had ordered a jeweled sword to wear at court, he managed to slip off with the valuable weapon. Saigo gave it away to a poor student. By his action, he meant to show Okubo the error of his ways. Such ostentation did not fit with the samurai ideals of simplicity and austerity. Okubo did not appreciate the gesture, and the relationship between two men became cool and formal.

As Saigo felt more and more out of step, he feared that the spirit of Japan would be lost. Despite his reverence for the emperor, he believed that Meiji's advisors, who ruled in his name, served him badly. Finally, finding himself in disagreement on a major issue in 1875, he resigned, going back to Satsuma again.

There, Saigo's spirits rose. He wrote a poem:

I have shaken off the dust of the world,
I have taken leave of rank and fame.
Now I can give myself wholeheartedly to joy in Nature,
The great creator of all things.

But to many he was still a national hero, and he could not escape the demands of that role. Students flocked to his doorstep. He inspired them with his own vision of Japan's greatness, stressing the samurai ideals. The government became concerned. Spies were sent to attend his school; they reported that Saigo was teaching dangerous ideas.

It is unlikely that Saigo himself was plotting a revolt. But matters soon moved beyond his control. While Saigo was out hunting with his beloved dogs, some of his students attacked the imperial arsenal at Kagoshima. The government declared them rebels.

There was now no turning back. Saigo accepted the role that fate had thrust upon him. At the beginning of 1877 he led his young, eager samurai on the march. As Saigo proceeded, the ranks of his army swelled. Others shared his devotion to the ancient samurai spirit. Old samurai, and even bands of women, the daughters of samurai clans, took up arms in the rebellion.

Saigo swept onward and arrived at the castle of Kumamoto in central Kyushu. Snow lay on the ground, for it was midwinter. Only a small garrison held the castle, and Saigo decided to capture it instead of going on. It was a mistake, for the fortress, built during Tokugawa Ieyasu's time, had thick walls that withstood Saigo's cannons. As the seige dragged on, it stalled Saigo's advance.

It is part of the tragic story that Saigo's old schoolmate Okubo now headed the government. He knew Saigo's character well. If Saigo was not stopped, he could threaten all the progress that the Meiji Restoration had accomplished. Okubo ordered a large force to lift the seige of Kumamoto.

The battle that followed was the first time that the new citizen army was tested against a samurai army. The fighting was bitter, but the modern training and weapons were decisive. The government forces managed to drive off Saigo's samurai army.

Saigo retreated south, his forces dwindling as he moved. By the time he reached Kagoshima he was down to a small group of faithful followers. When 30,000 government troops arrived, Saigo moved his headquarters into a cave on a hill north of the town.

Saigo knew he could not win, but he was serene in the face of death—a samurai to the end. He received a letter from his former colleague General Yamagata Aritomo asking him to "end the situation." Aritomo did not use the word "surrender," for he knew that a samurai never surrendered. Saigo told the messenger he had no reply. He prepared for death and exchanged farewell cups of sake with his officers.

The government troops attacked on the 24th of September, 1877. Saigo was hit by a stray bullet and seriously wounded. His closest aide, Beppo Shinsuke, lifted Saigo's heavy body, carrying him to safety. Saigo spoke his last words: "My dear Shinsuke, I think this place will do." He faced the direction of the Imperial Palace and thrust his sword into his stomach. With one expert stroke, Beppo cut off his head—the duty of a samurai's follower. This was the ceremony of *seppuku*, more popularly called *harakiri*. It was the final act of honor in a samurai's life. Though painful, seppuku took away the shame of defeat by showing that a samurai chose death at his own hands rather than surrender or be captured.

Beppo then ran to the battle, crying, "The great teacher is dead!" He and the rest of the samurai died in the fighting, refusing to surrender.

When Saigo's head was found, it was brought to General Yamagata, who looked at it with sorrow. He knew it was Saigo's own sense of duty that had brought him to this end. Many Japanese agreed. Though Saigo died a rebel, he entered that select group of tragic heroes that includes Yoshitsune. Saigo's character was regarded as more important than his actions.

Okubo met his own end six months later at the hands of a band of assassins who were avenging Saigo's death. In the years that followed, Saigo has become one of the most popular heroes of modern Japan. As he himself wrote, posterity honors the man who acts with sincerity. Today a statue of Saigo, dog at his side, stands in Ueno Park overlooking Tokyo. It is an ever-present reminder of the last samurai, and the samurai ideals of Japan.

CHAPTER 11

A TRAILBLAZER FOR WOMEN— HANI MOTOKO

Each morning as she walked to her teaching job, Matsuoka Motoko stopped at the employment offices of the Tokyo newspapers. Her real ambition was to be a journalist, a male profession in Meiji Japan. Motoko, however, refused to let that stand in her way. When she learned that the *Hochi* newspaper needed a copy editor, she decided to apply. She carefully prepared a resume and letter describing her qualifications and explaining the advantage of having a female copy editor. The next morning, she reached the newspaper office so early that only the janitor was present. "Are you applying for the opening yourself?" he asked. "A copy editor is a man's position, you know."

Motoko told a white lie. "No I was asked to deliver this to the person in charge," she responded. Her heart fell, for it looked as if her chances were slim.

But the next day, she received a postcard summoning her to an interview. As she sat in the small shabby waiting room, she noticed that several men were also applying for the position. She was the last to be interviewed. The editor agreed to consider her for the position if she would start a one-day trial right away. Motoko eagerly said yes, and immediately was whisked into the cubicle of the chief copy editor. He gave her some advertisements to proofread. At the end of the day, the chief smiled and said, "That's it for today. Come back around ten o'clock in the morning. You'll probably do." With joy in her heart, Motoko left the newspaper office. She was on her way.

Matsuoka Motoko was born on September 8, 1873, during the height of Japan's modernization. In the year of her birth Japan officially adopted the Western calendar and established a system of

compulsory education. Because she grew up in a time of such great change, Motoko often challenged traditions throughout her life.

Her hometown was Hachinohe, in the remote northeastern part of Honshu. Hachinohe had been a castle town, the headquarters of a daimyo who supplied horses for the Tokugawa shoguns. It was cold, rugged country, far from the comforts of Japan's major cities. Motoko's grandfather was a samurai whose only child was a daughter. When the girl married, Motoko's grandparents adopted her husband—a common practice to carry on the family name.

A woman's place in Japan was decidedly subordinate to men. In their home, Motoko and her mother had to wait until the men in the family had finished their meal before they could eat. Still, even as a young child, Motoko was strong willed and independent. Once, she left her umbrella by the roadside while she played. A passerby, thinking the umbrella was lost, took it to a nearby police station. Motoko marched indignantly into the station and demanded the umbrella. Her mother later heard that the police were still talking about the bold little girl.

Because the Meiji government opened schools for both boys and girls throughout the country, Motoko gained an advantage her mother never had. Motoko always remembered her first proud day of school, when she tucked her wooden name tag in the *obi* (sash) that bound her kimono. She entered the world of learning and her thirst for education became a lifelong quest. Even teasing by other students didn't dampen her enthusiasm. Early on, she developed a sense of self-reliance to help her overcome disappointment and hurt.

In Motoko's village school, boys and girls were separated until the fifth grade. After that, most girls dropped out, because their families believed girls needed only basic reading and writing skills. The boys teased the few girls who stayed, giving them silly nicknames. (Motoko's was "sweet roll.") By the eighth grade, Motoko was the only girl in her class, yet she was the star pupil.

At the age of 11, Motoko suffered through a family tragedy. Her father took a mistress and became involved with his brother's dishonest business dealings. When the police investigated, Motoko's grandfather acted to protect the family. On his orders, Motoko's parents were divorced. Her father could no longer bear the Matsuoka name. He remarried and stayed in the town. Motoko was torn between her love for him and the shame of the scandal.

After graduation, Motoko went on living at home and took English-language classes. There were few opportunities for women to obtain higher education in Japan, but Motoko's grandfather sympathized with her ambition. When he read in a newspaper about the opening of Tokyo's Women's Higher School, he enrolled Motoko. The school was the first publicly financed general-education high school for women in Japan.

Her grandfather decided to take Motoko to Tokyo himself. Enthusiastic about the changes sweeping Japan, he wanted to be part of the celebration of the new constitution. Setting out by sleigh across the snow in early 1889, Motoko and her grandfather headed for Tokyo.

They switched to a steamship and finally to a train for the last leg of the journey. "How exciting it was to see a train for the first time in my life!" she recalled. "I absorbed everything in sight with a sense of wonder and joy. Outside the train window, leaves were gleaming. The people in the crowded car were all strangers, each distinct from the other—so fascinating to a girl from a town where everyone knew everyone else."

They arrived in Tokyo in time for the presentation of the Meiji Constitution on February 11. The date was already a national holiday; it celebrated Jimmu's becoming the first emperor. Now, the Meiji emperor was offering a constitution as his gift to the people of Japan. The constitution recognized the emperor's divine status, describing him as "sacred and inviolable."

While waiting for school to open, Motoko's grandfather showed her around the capital city. As a young man, he had served at his daimyo's residence in Edo. But all the changes that had taken place since that time astonished him. The city had more than doubled in size since the emperor moved there. Trolley cars ran through the streets; electric lights lit up the Ginza, the business district; the old daimyos' estates had become public parks; and many people wore western clothing instead of kimonos. The city was headquarters for steamship lines, railways, and cotton and silk mills. (Many of these were financed by the Mitsui Bank, which funded the Tokyo Electric Light Company four years after Thomas Edison perfected the light bulb.)

Motoko loved the stimulating atmosphere of the bustling city. She moved into a boardinghouse with other female students. Though she studied hard, she also became drawn into the exciting events going on around her. The first session of the Imperial Diet, Japan's Congress, opened, but women did not have the right to vote for its members. Motoko became interested in the small movement for greater women's rights, and attended political meetings where women spoke. Still she studied hard to keep up her grades. After three years, she became part of the first graduating class of the women's high school.

She also began a quest for greater meaning within her personal life. A friend took her to a service in a Christian church. Drawn to the faith, Motoko was baptized.

Motoko hoped to go on to college, but all the ones that admitted women charged tuition. She did not want to ask her grandfather to pay. Instead, she found an opportunity to work her way through the Meiji Women's School by working on the school magazine, *Women's Learning*. Her years at the Meiji School increased Motoko's confidence and abilities. She worked with Japanese writers and translators, meeting many influential people. She copy edited the first Japanese translation of the English children's book, *Little*

Lord Fauntleroy. Inspired, she decided to make journalism her career.

So Motoko was thrilled to land the job with the *Hoshi* newspaper. On her first full day of work, her editor warned her, "As the first woman to work in our editing room, you will have to prove yourself." She accepted the challenge. Despite taunts from male co-workers in the beginning, her fine work gained their respect.

Not satisfied, Motoko still wanted to write her own articles. The newspaper had a column called "Portraits of Leading Women," which featured sketches of leading society ladies. Motoko recalled that one of her teachers at the Women's Higher School had been a tutor for the children of a noblewoman, Lady Tani. The teacher had often related the story of Lady Tani's experiences in the besieged Kumamoto Castle during Saigo's Rebellion. Motoko used her contact to obtain an interview with Lady Tani. The editor printed her article, making Motoko Japan's first woman reporter.

Soon her stories appeared on the front page of the paper. She investigated orphanages, hospitals, and other public institutions of Meiji Japan. Her reporting won respect for its research and fairness. Motoko's name became famous in Tokyo. While still in her mid-20s, she had opened the way to new careers for Japanese women. It was quite an achievement for a young woman from a remote northern province.

While working at the *Hochi*, Motoko fell in love with Hani Yashikazu, another journalist. Theirs was a modern relationship between two equals. With their marriage, a lifelong collaboration began. "Our home has been the center of our work," she later wrote, "and our work has been an extension of our home life: the two are completely merged....I am truly grateful for this ideal union that is the very essence of both our work and marriage. Together, we have found our place in life."

In 1908, the couple started a magazine called *Fujin no tomo*— "The Woman's Friend." The motto of the magazine was, "Daily life in itself is an education." Yashikazu was its business manager, and Motoko the editor. In fact, she wrote the entire contents of the first issue. "It must have been difficult," Motoko recalled, "but all I remember now is the excitement, not the difficulty."

Their magazine addressed women's problems and concerns, such as their new role in Japanese society, job opportunities, and their emotional lives. In its pages were articles about women's suffrage, consumer unions, agriculture, health problems, household budgets, marriage, and the education of children. Over time it branched out to discussions of world problems as well as domestic advice.

In 1921, Motoko and her husband decided to put their ideas into practice. They founded a school for girls, called the Jiyu Gakuen. The school's motto was, "Thinking, Living, Praying." Its goal was to educate the complete person, stressing both intellectual achievement and practical life, as well as developing self-awareness and independence. As director of the school, Motoko strove to combine the ideals of East and West. The school's first building was designed by the American architect Frank Lloyd Wright, but it shows strong Japanese influence.

Jiyu Gakuen means "Free School." Though it charged tuition, it was free from the strict rules set by the Japanese Ministry of Education. But *jiyu*, or freedom, also signified the spirit of the school—to free children to think for themselves. Motoko wrote that the goal of education should be to create a totally free individual. This was a revolutionary idea in 20th-century Japan, which valued duty to emperor and country.

The school accepted children of privileged families, but Motoko insisted that they perform ordinary tasks such as cleaning and cooking. After a boys' section was added in 1935, students built Japan's smallest hydroelectric plant on the campus, bred hogs and trout, and grew their own food on a nearby farm. Some of the students worked in child-care centers as part of their duties. The couple continued their work until their deaths. Motoko died in 1957, two years after her husband.

Hani Motoko blazed a trail for other women in modern Japan. She gained her achievements through her own efforts. She had the initiative and courage to seek a self-sufficient, productive life, when the usual course for women was to live in the shadow of their husbands. Her driving sense of mission made her believe that each woman could make a contribution to society. Her achievement continues today. The *Fujin no tomo* is still a popular women's magazine. The Jiyu Gakuen now enrolls students from kindergarten through college and is operated by the children of Hani Motoko.

C H A P T E R   1 2

SALESMAN TO THE WORLD— AKIO MORITA

While eating lunch on August 7, 1945, Akio Morita, a young Japanese navy officer, heard the terrifying news. The day before, the city of Hiroshima had been destroyed by a single bomb dropped from an American warplane. Morita, who had studied the science of physics in college, realized at once that only an atomic bomb could have caused that kind of damage.

Morita put down the bowl of rice he had been eating and turned to the other officers at the table. He told them, "We might as well give up our research right now. If the Americans can build an atomic bomb, we must be too far behind in every field to catch up."

Not everyone was so clearheaded as Morita. In its long history, Japan had never lost a war, and its military leaders were unwilling to accept defeat now. Some of them wanted to continue the war, even if it meant the complete destruction of Japan.

Three days later, a second atomic bomb destroyed the city of Nagasaki. Meanwhile, Akio Morita had obtained permission to visit his parents in the city of Nagoya. He considered it possible that he might never see them again.

Unknown to him, Emperor Hirohito was meeting with his advisers in a bomb shelter under the imperial palace in Tokyo. There, Hirohito sat silently for hours as his advisers argued. Should Japan continue to fight to preserve its honor? Or should it accept the terms of "unconditional surrender" that were offered?

At last, Hirohito rose to speak. Some of the men in the hot, stuffy bomb shelter wept as he told them that he could not bear to see his people suffer any longer. The emperor made his wishes clear: Japan must accept defeat. Late that night, Hirohito recorded a speech announcing his decision. At noon the next day, it would be broadcast on the national radio station.

Akio Morita's mother shook him awake that morning. The news that the emperor was going to speak on the radio had spread throughout the nation. It was a momentous event, for few Japanese had ever heard their emperor's voice. Many knelt before their radios to listen. As Morita himself described his actions, "[I] put on my full uniform, including my sword, and I stood at attention while we listened to the broadcast."

Even then, Morita was thinking about the future, when "Japan would need all the talent it could save....I felt that somehow I had a role to play in that future. I didn't know how big a role it would turn out to be."

On January 26, 1921, Kyuzaemon Morita had rejoiced when his wife Shuho gave birth to their first child, a son. The family name means "prosperous rice field," and for 300 years, the Moritas had been brewers of sake, the rice wine that is Japan's national drink. The wealthy family named their son Akio, which was written with the Japanese character for "enlightened."

Akio's mother came from a samurai family, and always wore a kimono in memory of her roots. Her husband, however, wore Western business suits to work and was very interested in the new technology coming from Western nations. The family had a General Electric washing machine and a Westinghouse refrigerator.

From early childhood, Akio was trained for the role he was expected to assume someday as head of the family business. "When I was as young as ten or eleven," he recalled, "I was first taken to... the sake brewery. I... had to sit at my father's side through long and boring board meetings....I was always told, 'You are the boss from the start. You are the eldest son in the family.'"

In due time, Akio might have followed his ancestors as head of the sake business. But the course of his life changed because his mother "was very fond of Western classical music and she bought many phonograph records for our old Victrola." The poor quality of the sound coming from the machine, which had to be wound up with a crank on the side, bothered Akio's father. He purchased a brand-new electric record player with vacuum tubes.

"I was absolutely astounded," recalled Akio. "I listened to our records over and over again—Mozart, Bach, Beethoven, Brahms— full of excitement and wonder that an electrical device like the vacuum tube could take the same old scratchy, hissing records we knew so well and make them sound so marvelous."

"Obsessed with this new discovery," Akio devoted all his time to learning more about electronics. He borrowed books and subscribed to magazines, both Japanese and foreign. He built his own radio and phonograph. Spending so much time on his electronic experiments almost caused Akio to flunk out of school. His parents worried that he would not pass the tough examinations to get into high school. But Akio buckled down to study hard and squeaked past the exams. In high school, he excelled in science, and he was studying physics at Osaka University when World War II began.

Morita enlisted in the navy, which assigned him to a research center working on heat-seeking devices. There he met Masaru Ibuka, a civilian who headed a company that made precise measurement devices for radar. Though Ibuka was 13 years older than Morita, the two men formed a close friendship that would someday result in one of the greatest businesses in the world.

That day was still far away at the end of the war. Japan was occupied by American troops. Though Emperor Hirohito was permitted to keep his throne, he had to give up his status as a *kami*, or god. In fact, the most powerful man in the country was General Douglas MacArthur, the Supreme Commander of the Allied Occupation Forces. MacArthur, nicknamed "the American shogun," wrote a new constitution for Japan, giving it a democratic form of government. In the constitution, Japan turned its back on its military tradition by renouncing war "forever."

With much of its industry destroyed by bombs, Japan was desperately poor. Masaru Ibuka formed a new company, called Tokyo Telecommunications Research Laboratories. It was a grand name for a business that occupied a small office in a bombed-out department store and had no products to sell. Even so, when Ibuka offered his wartime friend a partnership, Morita was excited.

Morita was teaching at the Tokyo Institute of Technology, but knew that his father still expected him to take over the family business. So Morita brought Ibuka to meet Kyuzaemon Morita. "In Japan," Akio wrote, "it was considered a serious thing to take a son, especially a first son, out of his home and family environment...In some cases, it was almost as though an adoption was taking place." After listening to Ibuka explain his plans for the business, however,

Morita's father gave his consent. In fact, he loaned the new business money to keep it going in its early days—one of the best investments ever made.

Ibuka and Morita soon found themselves in competition with older and larger companies. Ibuka wanted to produce something that no one else was making. While delivering some equipment to the national radio station, he saw that product—an American tape recorder. He realized that it was a great improvement on the old wire recorders, and Morita agreed. They set out to build one.

Their biggest problem was making the thin plastic tape itself, which was not available in Japan. Finally they cut long strips of paper, laid them out on the laboratory floor, and experimented with different kinds of magnetic coating. They cooked batches of the coating in a frying pan to find the right formula, and then spread it on the tape with brushes made of raccoon hairs.

In 1950, Morita and Ibuka put their first tape recorders on the market. "We were in for a rude awakening," recalled Morita. "We could not sell it." Analyzing the problem, he realized that people saw no use for such an expensive product—160,000 yen, or almost $500. So Morita became a salesman. Learning that court stenographers were in demand because few were trained during the war, he demonstrated the tape recorder for Japan's Supreme Court. He received an order for 20 of the 50 machines he and Ibuka had built.

The company was on its way to success, but Morita had learned an important lesson: "Having unique technology and being able to make unique products are not enough to keep a business going. You have to sell the products, and to do that you have to show the potential buyer the real value of what you are selling." He took over the duties of merchandising the company's products, while Ibuka concentrated on product design.

In 1948 Ibuka and Morita learned about a new electronic device invented at Bell Laboratories in the United States. Called a transistor, it could amplify sound. The first ones, however, were used only for specialized scientific instruments. In 1953, when Morita went to the United States to obtain a license to use the transistor, he was told that hearing aids were the only consumer products that it was useful for.

Morita and Ibuka had another idea—to use it for making miniature radios. As Morita wrote, this was a natural idea, for

"Miniaturization and compactness have always appealed to the Japanese. Our boxes have been made to nest; our fans fold; our art rolls into neat scrolls." Morita set a goal of making a radio that would be small enough to fit into a shirt pocket.

It took four years to reach that goal, and Ibuka had to make key improvements in the transistor along the way. Meanwhile, he and Morita talked about putting a new company name on their radio. While Morita was in the United States, he found that nobody could pronounce the name of their company in Japanese, and even the English translation was difficult. The partners

wanted a new name that could be recognized anywhere in the world, one that could be pronounced the same in any language. We made dozens and dozens of tries. Ibuka and I went through dictionaries looking for a bright name, and we came across the Latin word *sonus*, meaning "sound." The word itself seemed to have sound in it. Our business was full of sound, so we began to zero in on *sonus*. At that time in Japan borrowed English slang and nicknames were becoming popular and some people referred to bright, young and cute boys as "sonny," or "sonny-boys," and of course "sunny" and "sonny".... Unfortunately the single word "sonny" by itself would give us troubles in Japan because [it] would be pronounced "sohnnee," which means to lose money. That was no way to launch a new product. We pondered this problem for a little while and the answer struck me one day: why not just drop one of the letters and make it "Sony"? That was it!

The company's name was changed to Sony in January 1958. Since then, it has appeared in over 170 countries. As everybody knows, the miniature radio was an enormous success, and the seemingly endless stream of new products that followed has made Sony one of the most successful companies in the world.

Sony's products have been known for their high quality and technological innovations. For example the first color television sets, made in the United States, used three electronic "guns" that projected electrons onto a screen. Each gun provided a different color—red, blue, and green. Sony's technicians invented a single-gun system that made the picture sharper and clearer, and Sony's Trinitron captured the market from American television makers.

Morita himself came up with the idea for one of Sony's best-known products—the Walkman portable cassette player. Even so, most of his technicians and salespeople doubted that it would sell. In Japanese businesses, decisions are not handed down from the top. Everyone contributes to the process, and Morita had to argue quite strongly to persuade the others. "It embarrassed me to be so excited about a product most others thought would be a dud," he recalled. "But I was so confident...that I said I would take personal responsibility for the project. I never had reason to regret it."

One of Sony's few failures was its videocassette recorder, called the Betamax. Though it was first on the consumer market, other companies soon jumped in, using a different kind of tape system called VHS. It turned out that most people wanted to use videocassette recorders to watch movies—and the VHS makers had licensed the right to make tape copies of most of the available movies. Though Morita insisted the Beta system was technologically superior, the VHS recorders are now the standard type.

The Betamax failure taught Morita another lesson: hardware, the machine itself, would sell only when it was combined with popular software, the programs used by the machine. It was for this reason that Sony made two of its most spectacular business decisions. In 1987 the company spent $2 billion to buy CBS Records, which had a huge catalog of music from classical to Michael Jackson. Two years later, Sony also acquired Columbia Pictures, an American movie and television studio, at a cost of $3.4 billion.

Morita had made sure that his company now controlled a leading maker of software for any new products in the future. And

there were plenty of those in development: a new eight-millimeter videocassette format; digital-tape recording, which can make tapes that sound as good as CDs; and high-definition television (HDTV), which promises to bring movielike clarity to home TV sets.

As Sony grew, so did many other Japanese companies. After the disaster of World War II, the Japanese people turned their talents and energies to building high-quality products. Sales of Japanese automobiles, computers, and electronic products have made Japan an economic superpower, the equal of the United States and of the combined European countries.

Japan's economic success has sometimes caused tensions with the United States, where many workers have lost their jobs because American industries could not compete with Japanese products. Akio Morita, who has become better known than any Japanese politician, has become a goodwill ambassador for his country. Morita has lived for several years in the United States and even sent his children to school here. He has written books and articles to explain and defend the Japanese way of doing business.

Morita points out that Japanese companies have opened factories in this country, providing new jobs. Forty percent of all Sony employees are now non-Japanese. Morita complains, however, that Americans "are always in a hurry." He contrasts this with Sony's long-term view:

> We have been working on HDTV for more than 10 years because we are not satisfied with today's TV standard....It's just like digital recording, the technology used in compact disks. When we started working on it 20 years ago, we didn't think, "We're going to make compact disks." We were seeking new... technology that would produce better recordings.

Morita knows that technology is a means to an end. He has not forgotten the thrill he felt when he first heard an electric phonograph more than 60 years ago. That sense of fun still drives him:

> Every week, I take a new product to my home to use—to play with, just like a layman. That's how I find what we should improve. I read the instruction manuals. Sometimes I cannot understand how to use the machine! The product should be loved by the customers. That's how we can enrich their lives.

G L O S S A R Y

Aware: The pathos or sorrow one feels on beholding beautiful things; an important esthetic principle of Japanese art.

Bakufu: Military government that ruled Japan during most of the period between 1192 and 1868.

Buddhism: A religion started in India by Siddhartha Gautama (known as the Buddha) in the sixth century B.C. It spread to Japan after A.D. 552.

Bushido: The code of honor followed by the samurai, who were called bushi in earlier times.

Chanoyu: The tea ceremony.

Confucianism: A philosophy and way of life based on the teachings of Confucius, a Chinese scholar who lived in the sixth century B.C. It spread to Japan during the regency of Prince Shotoku.

Daimyo: A lord; independent daimyos controlled large portions of the country before the unification of Japan under Tokugawa Ieyasu in 1600.

Floating world: The pleasure district of a Japanese city.

Geisha: Woman trained in the arts of conversation, singing, and playing musical instruments.

Haiku: A poem composed in three lines of five, seven, and five syllables.

Imperial regalia: The sword, jewel, and mirror—by legend, the gifts of the Sun Goddess, Amaterasu—that are the symbols of the Japanese emperor's right to rule.

Jiri: The sacred duty of a samurai, which he was obliged to fulfill even if it meant his death.

Kabuki: The form of dance-theater developed by Okuni. The name conveys the idea of something slightly improper.

Kabukimono: Fans of kabuki theater who were known for their rebellious, nonconforming behavior.

Kagura: The sacred Shinto dance.

Kami: Spirits or gods in the ancient Japanese religion of nature-worship. By tradition, the emperor was a kami because he was directly descended from the Sun Goddess, Amaterasu.

Kamikaze: "Divine wind," the typhoon that wrecked the Mongol fleet that invaded Japan in 1281. Japanese believed it was sent by the gods as a sign of their favor.

Kampaku: Military ruler, a title taken by those who were by birth ineligible for the title of shogun.

Kana: Simplified version of the Chinese written characters; developed for the writing of Japanese in the ninth century.

Lotus Sutra: One of the most important scriptures, or texts, of Buddhism. The monk Nichiren emphasized its importance in the form of Buddhism he developed.

Manga: "Irresponsible pictures," the name Hokusai used for his humorous, satirical sketches. Today's Japanese comic books are also called manga.

Meiji Restoration: The seizure of political power by the followers of the Meiji emperor in 1868. It ended the 700-year period of bakufu rule, or military government.

Namban: "Southern barbarians," a name used by Japanese for all Europeans.

Ninja: "Invisible person," a specially trained fighter who carried out secret missions, such as assassinations.

No drama: A form of theater popular among Japanese nobility.

Samurai: A warrior; during the era of the Tokugawa shoguns, the samurai formed the highest class in Japanese society.

Satori: The state of enlightenment that was the goal of those who followed the Buddhist religion.

Seppuku: Ritual suicide that a samurai was obliged to follow to avoid surrender or defeat. Also called hara-kiri.

Shinto: The ancient Japanese religion of nature-worship.

Shogun: Military dictator who ruled in the emperor's name.

Tatami: A straw mat used on the floors of Japanese homes.

Tempura: Vegetables or meat dipped in batter and deep-fried. This form of cooking was brought to Japan by Portuguese.

Tenno: The emperor of Japan.

Tokonoma: The alcove of a room or hut in which the tea ceremony was held. By custom, a work of art or other beautiful object was displayed in the tokonama.

Ukiyo-e: Wood-block prints that were popular in Japan from the mid-eighteenth century on.

Waka: A five-line poem composed by two people in sequence.

BIBLIOGRAPHY

Aoki, Michiko, and Dardress, Margret B., eds., *As the Japanese See It Past and Present*, Honolulu: University of Hawaii Press, 1981.

Baker, Joan Stanley, *Japanese Art*, London: Thames and Hudson, 1984.

Basho, *The Narrow Road to the Deep North*, trans. Nobuyuki Yuasa, New York: Penguin Books, 1986.

Beard, Mary R., *The Force of Women in Japanese History*, Washington, D.C.: Public Affairs Press, 1953.

de Bary, William Theodore, ed., *The Buddhist Tradition in India, China and Japan*, New York: Vintage Books, 1972.

Frederic, Louis, *Daily Life in Japan at the Time of the Samurai, 1185-1603*, New York: Praeger, 1972.

Frost, Peter K., *The Golden Age of China and Japan*, Columbus, OH: Charles E. Merrill Publishing Co., 1971.

Henderson, Harold G., ed., *An Introduction to Haiku*, Garden City, NY: Doubleday Anchor Books, 1958.

Hoobler, Dorothy and Thomas, *Showa: The Age of Hirohito*, New York: Walker & Co., 1990.

Hoover, Thomas, *Zen Culture*, New York: Random House, 1977.

Keene, Donald, ed., *Anthology of Japanese Literature from the Earliest Era to the Mid-Nineteenth Century*, New York: Grove Press, 1955.

Keene, Donald, *Travelers of a Hundred Ages*, New York: Henry Holt and Co., 1989.

Mason, A.H.P., and Caiger, J.G., *A History of Japan*, Tokyo: Charles E. Tuttle Co., 1972.

Michener, James A., *The Floating World*, Honolulu: University of Hawaii Press, 1983.

Morita, Akio, *Made in Japan*, New York: Dutton, 1986.

Morris, Ivan, trans., *The Pillow Book of Sei Shonagon*, Baltimore: Penguin Books, 1971.

Morris, Ivan, *The Nobility of Failure: Tragic Heroes in the History of Japan*, New York: Holt, Rinehart, and Winston, 1975.

Morris, Ivan, *The World of the Shining Prince*, New York: Penguin Books, 1964.

Mulhern, Chieko Irie, ed., *Heroes With Grace: Legendary Women of Japan*, Armonk, NY: M.E. Sharpe, Inc., 1991.

Murasaki, Lady, *The Tale of Genji*, trans. by Arthur Waley, New York: Modern Library, 1960.

Narazaki, Muneshige, ed., *Hokusai, "The Thirty-Six Views of Mt. Fuji,"* Tokyo: Kodansha International, 1968.

Nishida, Kazuo, *Storied Cities of Japan*, Tokyo: Weatherhill, 1963.

Okakura, Kakuzo, *The Book of Tea*, Tokyo: Kodansha, 1989.

Omori, Annie Shepley and Kochi, Doi, trans., *Diaries of Court Ladies of Old Japan*, New York: AMS Press, 1970.

Roberts, John G., *Mitsui: Three Centuries of Japanese Business*, Tokyo: Weatherhill, 1973.

Sansom, G.B., *Japan: A Short Cultural History*, New York: Appleton-Century-Crofts, 1962.

Schirokauer, Conrad, *A Brief History of Chinese and Japanese Civilizations*, New York: Harcourt Brace Jovanovich, 1978.

Tsunoda, Ryusaku, de Bary, William Theodore, and Keene, Donald, compilers, *Sources of Japanese Tradition*, New York: Columbia University Press, 1958.

Turnbull, Stephen, *Samurai Warriors*, Poole, Dorset, England: Blandford Press, 1987.

Varley, H. Paul, *Japanese Culture*, Honolulu: University of Hawaii Press, 1984.

S O U R C E S

Introduction: A Divine Land
page 4: "This god had..." Tsunoda, Ryusaku, et. al., Sources of Japanese Tradition, p. 19.
page 5: "Do Thou, my August Grandchild..." Ibid., p. 20.

Chapter 1: Prince Shotoku Taichi
page 7: "He was able..." Tsunoda, op.cit., p. 45.
page 8: "Though difficult..." Frost, Peter K., The Golden Age of China and Japan, p. 13.
page 8: "Why should we revere..." Mason, A.H.P., A History of Japan, p. 22.
pages 9-10: "Let us cease..." Baker, Joan Stanley, Japanese Art, p. 261.
page 11: "At this time..." Tsunoda, op.cit., p. 48.

Chapter 2: Lady Murasaki and Sei Shonagon

page 12: "A very proud person...." Beard, Mary R., The Force of Women in Japanese History, pp. 131-132.

pages 12, 14: "Having no excellence..." Ibid., p. 132.

page 15: "His resplendent..." Schirokauer, Conrad, A Brief History of Chinese and Japanese Civilizations, p. 163.

page 15: "On that day..." Baker, op.cit., p. 83.

page 16: "I now had a vast..." Morris, Ivan, trans., The Pillow Book of Sei Shonagon, pp. 10-11.

page 16: "In spring it is..." Ibid., p. 21.

page 17: "One day when he thought..." Mason, op.cit., 70.

page 17: "One has gone to bed..." Morris, op.cit., p. 46.

page 17: "I hurried..." Ibid., p. 244.

page 18: "When my elder brother..." Keene, Donald, ed., Anthology of Japanese Literature, p. 155.

page 18: "Do they really look..." Keene, Donald, Travelers of a Hundred Ages, p. 46.

page 19: "I wish I could..." Omori, Annie Shepley, and Doi, Kochi, trans., Diaries of Court Ladies of Old Japan, p. 94.

page 20: "As Genji danced..." Morris, Ivan, The World of the Shining Prince, p. 202.

page 20: "...it happens because..." Lady Murasaki, The Tale of Genji, Waley, Arthur, trans., p. 501.

Chapter 3: Yoritomo and Yoshitsune

page 25: "Elated with victory..." Mason, op.cit., p. 100.

page 26: "The Emperor was seven..." Keene, Anthology, op. cit., p. 184.

page 26: "On the twenty-fourth..." Morris, Ivan, The Nobility of Failure, p. 77.

page 26: "Here am I..." Sansom, G.B., Japan: A Short Cultural History, p. 293.

Chapter 4: Nichiren

page 29: "When I, Nichiren..." Tsunoda, op.cit., p. 226.

pages 29-30: "Nichiren, reciting the Scripture..." Frederic, Louis, Daily Life in Japan at the Time of the Samurai, pp. 201-202.

page 32: "If you desire..." de Bary, William Theodore, ed., The Buddhist Tradition, pp. 349-350.

page 33: "I shall be the pillar..." Frederic, op.cit., p. 202.

Chapter 5: Sen no Rikyu

page 39: "He resembled..." Turnbull, Stephen, Samurai Warriors, p. 108.

page 41: "Never again..." Okakura, Kakuzo, The Book of Tea, p. 132,

Chapter 6: Okuni

page 46: "They wear rosaries..." Schirokauer, op.cit., p. 313.

page 46: "Of all among..." Mulhern, Chieko Irie, ed. Heroic With Grace, p. 19.

page 46: "...threw away their wealth..." Schirokauer, p. 133.

Chapter 7: Mitsui Shuho
page 50: "A great peace..." Roberts, John G., Mitsui, p. 12.

Chapter 8: Basho
page 54: "Many, many things..." Henderson, Harold G., ed. An Introduction to Haiku, p. 17.
page 56: "An ancient pond..." Hoover, Thomas, Zen Culture, p. 10.
page 57: "Everything about me..." Keene, Travelers, op.cit., p. 309.
page 57: "The months and days..." Keene, Anthology, op.cit., p. 361.
page 58: "The summer grasses..." Mason, op.cit., p. 197.
page 58: "The conflict has waged..." Keene, Travelers, op.cit., p. 301.
page 58: "Seized with a disease..." Basho, The Narrow Road to the Deep North, p. 47.

Chapter 9: Hokusai
page 59: "I have created..." Nishida, Kazuo, Storied Cities of Japan, p. 152.
page 61: "Living only for..." Baker, op.cit., p. 186.
page 61: "I suggest..." Michener, James A., The Floating World, p. 154.
page 64: "A horse might..." Narazaki, Muneshige, ed. Hokusai: "The Thirty-Six Views of Mt. Fuji," p. 16.
page 65: "From the age of six..." Baker, op.cit., pp. 188-189.
page 65: "If heaven would only..." Michener, op.cit., p. 195.

Chapter 10: Saigo Takemori
pages 69-70: "Clasped in each other's..." Morris, Ivan, The Nobility of Failure, p. 235.
page 71: "A man of true sincerity..." Ibid., p. 243.
page 72: "I have shaken off..." Ibid., p. 158.

Chapter 11: Hani Motoko
page 74: job application, Mulhern, op.cit., p. 255.
page 77: "I absorbed everything..." Aoki, Michiko, ed., As the Japanese See It, p. 141.
page 79: "As the first woman..." Mulhern, op. cit., p. 256.
page 79: "Our home has been..." Mulhern, op.cit., p. 233.

Chapter 12: Akio Morita
All quotes from Morita, Akio, Made in Japan, pp. 3, 4, 12, 14, 16, 47, 58, 70, 66.

INDEX